MOHANDAS GANDHI

Handwritten annotations (top):

Darwinism · Wants change →
Industrialism
Optimism for absolute still
Women
Oppression

His theory is modern.
[See him affecting 20th.c.]
← Passive Resistance

MODERN MASTERS

Spirit of an Age →

Already published

ALBERT CAMUS / Conor Cruise O'Brien

FRANTZ FANON / David Caute

HERBERT MARCUSE / Alasdair MacIntyre

CHE GUEVARA / Andrew Sinclair

CLAUDE LÉVI-STRAUSS / Edmund Leach

LUDWIG WITTGENSTEIN / David Pears

GEORGE LUKÁCS / George Lichtheim

NOAM CHOMSKY / John Lyons

JAMES JOYCE / John Gross

MARSHALL MCLUHAN / Jonathan Miller

GEORGE ORWELL / Raymond Williams

SIGMUND FREUD / Richard Wollheim

WILLIAM BUTLER YEATS /
Denis Donoghue

WILHELM REICH / Charles Rycroft

Handwritten annotations (right):

Characteristics that prevailed

Freedom
↓
Rel. of MEN + women

Handwritten annotations (bottom):

Archaeology.
(Feminist attitude.
F.L. Women.

MODERN MASTERS

EDITED BY frank kermode

mohandas gandhi

george woodcock

NEW YORK | THE VIKING PRESS

CONTENTS

MOHANDAS GANDHI

i

In 1970, during the tense, nervous days before the breaking of the monsoon, mobs of Naxalite terrorists roamed the streets of Calcutta. They burned buses, killed policemen and school-teachers, wrecked cinemas showing anti-Chinese films, and sacked American agencies and university offices. But the most frequent targets of their attacks were the Gandhian centers dedicated to the uplift of urban populations. Gandhi's writings were burned; his portraits were destroyed.

Milton once described the destruction of a book as "a kind of homicide," and these acts of the Naxalites in 1970 reminded one that, more than twenty years before, the writer of the volumes they destroyed had himself been murdered by another group of fanatics devoted to a narrow vision of the desirable future. The men who killed Gandhi in 1948 were Hindu terrorists who objected to his insistence that liberated India must treat men of all religions with equal justice and generosity. The Naxalites, condemning his teachings as "the crystallization of revisionism," were seeking to weaken the appeal of the only revolutionary tradition other than Communism that has made an impression on the minds of the Indian masses.

Their actions demonstrated something more than the contrast between their views of social change and those formulated and lived out by Gandhi. They also showed that, even if Gandhi left no party to carry on his tradition and is now honored in memory rather than action by Indian governments, the myth created by his teaching, his example, his charismatic presence, is still potent in the slums and villages of India. In ghastly oleograph, his portrait is often seen beside that of Lord Krishna on the mud walls of Indian hovels, and among the illiterate his name is still mentioned in the tones proper when one speaks of an avatar.

Gandhi, indeed, has become petrified in Indian popular memory as the great culture hero of the recent past, an Arjuna with the outward appearance of a Hanuman. This man of punctilious honesty and rather demonstrative modesty, who resented the title of Mahatma or Great Soul conferred unasked upon him by Rabindranath Tagore, has left a name with which politicians and publicists still play dishonestly. They use it to justify, to a peasantry who remember Gandhi as the man who gave hope and self-respect, a modern India whose social and political ways have little relation to his beliefs and actions. What is lasting in Gandhi's achievement has to be considered apart from those who proclaim themselves his official heirs, and that is appropriate, for Gandhi was a completely unofficial man. He recognized the gulf that lay between the enjoyment of freedom and the exercise of authority. When the Indian National Congress, which he had led intermittently as a movement dedicated to achieving liberation by legal and extra-legal means, itself grasped for power and became a political party, he withdrew. With an extraordinary persistence he made and kept himself one of the few free men of our time.

No man, of course, did more than Gandhi to achieve the liberation of India; no man did more to bring about the general end of the Empire. Thus, before his death, he had succeeded in one of his great aims; he had made sure that, even if India were to be governed badly, it would be governed at least by Indians. But it was a divided land, with most of the Moslems living in the separate state of Pakistan, that came out of independence, and even in the regions that remained to become modern India Gandhi was forced to recognize "that the social order of our dreams cannot come through the Congress party of today." Seeing violence all around him, observing the rise of corruption that frightened him, he felt often, in those last days of 1946 and 1947 as he strove for amity between Hindus and Moslems, that he had failed indeed.

Gandhi's sense of failure at the point of India's liberation, and the disillusionment of those who today observe India and compare it with the Spartan commonwealth of renewed villages that he envisioned, are both appropriate reactions (though, as I shall seek to show, they do not take account of the totality of his achievement). For Gandhi was a political activist, judging his theories by their results. What he thought, he tested in practice. Practice in turn helped to shape his thought, so that he could talk with accuracy of his career as a series of "experiments with Truth."

It was an existential pattern of thought and deed rather than a system of political or moral philosophy that Gandhi left behind him. His writings were indeed voluminous; they fill many volumes of the pious collections his followers have published since his death. But they were almost all occasional pieces, written often in the heat of action to be published in propaganda sheets; even his autobiography, *My Experiments with Truth*, appeared first as a serial in such a paper, and was intended to aid and inspire others by the example of his own search for truth through action. Intentions and theories meant nothing to him until they had been tested in the clash and conflict of life. "I seek my peace among disorders," he once said.

Gandhi was the first of the great activist theoreticians who changed the shape of our world and the form of our thought during the present century. In 1894, nine years before Lenin gathered his Bolshevik faction within the Russian Social Democratic Party, and a quarter of a century before Mao Tse-tung embraced the revolution as a way of life, Gandhi began his activities among the Indians who lived a marginal and oppressed existence as merchants and indentured laborers in South Africa. Combining thought with experience, he devised his own techniques of struggle arising out of the actual circumstances there, and in 1906, only three years after the Bolsheviks stepped on to the stage of history and a year after the first Russian Revolution of 1905, he announced his pioneer *Satyagraha* campaign, developing nonviolent resistance as a discipline of social struggle.

Satyagraha, the combination of two Gujarati words meaning truth and force, was a doctrine developed out of action and leading to action. It was the construction of a curiously concrete mind, attuned to the constantly changing relations between man and man, and between men and the world. One of the few points about Gandhi on which I found most Indians in agreement is his extreme realism. It was not merely that as a matter of principle he always tried to integrate idea and act; not merely that he believed it dishonest to preach and not practice. It was also that he looked at situations with the judicious eye of a lawyer and the shrewd eye of an Indian Bania, and emerged from his observation with solutions that appeared to be highly original but in fact were very practical and appropriate to the circumstances.

Many of Gandhi's proposals, which to outsiders seemed absurd and faddish, and which contributed to the alien view of him as a special kind of inspired clown, were completely sensible in the setting of the India he was attempting to elevate into self-respect and freedom. To revive the craft of spinning, which Indian peasants had ceased practicing before the last years of the nineteenth century, was much more than an act of antiquarian sentiment. It was an effective way of drawing attention to a whole group of conditions that needed changing: the virtual extinction of Indian village crafts; the fact that because there were no crafts the peasants were unemployed four months every year; the final appalling fact that their cash income was so minute that even a few rupees earned spinning yarn in the idle season would increase it notably.

An eye singularly cleansed of prejudice enabled Gandhi often to act in such a way as to dissolve prejudice in others. The progress made toward ending untouchability in India has been mainly the result of his work and that of his close disciples. When he attended his first meeting of the Indian National Congress in 1901, he found himself in a gathering of caste Hindus to which no untouchables had been admitted. The latrines, traditionally cleaned by those outside the class structure, were appallingly filthy. Gandhi did more than criticize; he took a brush in his hand and, in an act that itself constituted a revolution among caste Hindus seventy years ago, himself cleaned the latrine he proposed to use. He continued to clean latrines for the rest of his life, and in doing so he not merely demonstrated against untouchability and its humiliating consequences, but also gave practical expression to his conviction that sanitation (with its symbolic connotation of inner purification) was a most urgent need among the Indian masses.

Practicality (which helped him to forge original techniques of revolutionary action) and lack of prejudice (which brought him a following and a breadth of acceptance unprecedented in India with its divisions of caste and language and religion) combined in Gandhi with an exceptional insight into the power of symbolic actions to move men's minds, and with—as Nehru remarked—"a curious knack for doing the right thing at the psychological moment." To tramp—as he did in 1930—a couple of hundred miles through the summer dust of Indian country roads, with a lonely beach as his destination, and there to pick up a fleck of forbidden salt and defy an unreasonable law; it was a simple, poetic act, but it united the Indian people more than any act by any man before, and it hastened the end of an empire.

Gandhi owed much of his influence to the fact that he was regarded by many Indians as a holy man. He claimed to be a Hindu, but he also said on occasion that he was a Christian, a Buddhist, and a Jew as well, and hymns from all religions were sung at the prayer meetings that were regular features of his nonviolent campaigns as well as of his daily life in the ashrams he shared with his disciples. As a Hindu, in fact, he was very unorthodox, and much of his life he spent trying to eliminate the built-in abuses of Hinduism, such as the caste rules and child marriage. He was not a practicing mystic; he never claimed—though he longed for—inward religious experience. Yet much in his career remains unexplained if we forget his insistence that religion and politics were bound inextricably in the common search for Truth. "To me," he said, "Truth is God and there is no way to find truth except the way of nonviolence."

Truth conceived as God is of course the Absolute. Truth perceived by man must always be relative, changing according to human contacts, developing as men understand better each other, their circumstances, and themselves. Gandhi never set out to develop a fixed and final doctrine, but emphasized that his practice of ahimsa, or nonviolence, was always experimental, that his political struggle like his personal life was part of a continuing quest for Truth as manifested existentially, a quest that could never end because human understanding was incapable of comprehending the Absolute.

The identification of Truth as the goal of political action, as well as of religious devotion, and the refusal to distinguish between religion and politics, form the background to the great divergences between Gandhi's revolutionary ideas and techniques and those of other contemporary revolutionaries. Unlike the Marxists, he refused to accept any kind of determinist view of history. Man, in his view, was a free spirit, and nothing could

compel him to do what he did not will. Unorthodox
though he might be, Gandhi fitted into the traditional
pattern of the sannyasi, who practices nonattachment
in the search for Truth; he was the karma yogi, the man
who perfects and purifies himself through action. Yogic
disciplines of all kinds are held in India to confer
power over destiny, and Gandhi believed that positive
action—love and nonviolence—could intangibly influence men and therefore events.

With Truth as the goal and at the same time as the
principle of action (for in Gandhian terms ends are
emergent from means and hence virtually indis-
tinguishable from them) there was no place in Gandhi's
idea of revolution for conspiratorial methods or guerrilla
activities. Everything must be done openly, since the aim
of *Satyagraha* is not only to confront but also to convert
the enemy; to win him rather than harm him. The effect
of this kind of open revolutionary politics, as practiced
by Gandhi, was to draw the liberation movement into
close identity with the masses of people in all classes
and communities. At the same time, the peculiar stresses
of nonviolent action demanded the development among
the small core of "volunteers" or militant activists
of a discipline as rigorous as that of any guerrilla
movement.

The close identity with the masses, which made the
Gandhian movement of the 1920s and '30s a "going to
the people" far more effective and widespread than that
of the nineteenth-century Russian narodniks, was important for another reason. Like the Marxists and the
anarchists, Gandhi believed that society must be transformed, but unlike them he did not believe that it was
necessary to await an apocalyptic day of the revolution
before the transformation could begin. Indeed, he be-

lieved that the political revolution was dependent on the social transformation, and that both must proceed together. He held that, like spiritual liberation, the attainment of political freedom would only become a reality through self-purification, and it was his belief that Indian society must purge itself of its injustices before a true liberation from the imperial past would be possible. Rule by Indians would merely be a continuation of imperial rule in a slightly different form if it were not accompanied by an end to caste disabilities and a renewal of the village life followed by eight Indians out of every ten.

But it was not merely a question of changing social forms, of reviving village institutions and industries, of decentralizing administration and localizing authority, of creating a system of basic education, of liberating women from purdah, though all of these were among Gandhi's avowed objectives. Gandhi preached a total revolution and, since a society is no better than its members, the uplift of individuals was just as important as the transformation of their community. This view led Gandhi to extend his "experiments with Truth" into every field of living, and it is on this level of the personal revolution that we encounter those notions of diet and medicine and sexual behavior, and those slightly inhuman attitudes toward intimate human relationships, which often repelled Western observers and led even George Orwell to admit an "aesthetic distaste" for Gandhi.

When we watch Gandhi—our imaginations stimulated by his own vivid self-analyses—plastering mud poultices on his belly, and cheating his conscience by drinking goats' milk after he had taken a vow not to touch cows' milk, and testing his vow of brahmacharya, or continence, as an old man by sharing a bed with his grandniece, we can easily regard him as an eccentric who happened to be also a political genius. But the links between his personal fads and his political methods turn out to be logical; his steady pursuit of personal rigors helped him achieve a discipline rare among the Indians of his time, and this in turn allowed him to pursue his political activities with an imperturbable courage. And if he was a difficult husband, a negligent father by ordinary standards, and a moral tyrant over his disciples, these failings from a normal standpoint can be interpreted as manifestations of the doctrine of nonattachment which he consistently reinforced by his religious speculations, and which he as consistently applied to his political actions so that—as Krishna adjured Arjuna in Gandhi's favorite book, the Bhagavad Gita—they might be carried out without hope of reward.

In material terms he succeeded, though one may at times suspect that the "fruits of action" were in fact gathered in the shape of a formidable spiritual pride. Yet on the whole one has to agree with Orwell's final remark, after rejecting so many of Gandhi's theories and attitudes: "regarded simply as a politician, and compared with the other leading political figures of our time, how clean a smell he has managed to leave behind!" Despite his extraordinary political abilities, Gandhi remained uncorrupted in a country where politics and corruption have become almost synonymous. He not only lived in exemplary poverty and refused to favor his family according to traditional Indian kinship loyalties; he even denied himself the pleasure of triumphing over his enemies, by trying to make every settlement a face-saving compromise. Most important, whenever the chance of political power lay near at hand, before or after the liberation of India, he rejected it, and in this he was unique among the colonial rebels of his time or indeed among revolutionaries at any time. He confessed to being "a kind of anarchist," but it was a religious rather than a political impulse that held him back from authority, a knowledge that in the circumstances of India's liberation, political power and the way of ahimsa were incompatible.

It was at this point that Gandhi realized the extent of his isolation within the immense following that the struggle for liberation had brought him. Most of the political activists who had supported him against the British had done so merely because they found his tactics effective in achieving independence with a minimum of bloodshed, not because they accepted the principles on which these methods were based. "Nonviolence is my creed," he admitted sadly in those days when victory seemed to collapse into personal defeat. "It was never the way of Congress. With the Congress it had always been a policy."

Gandhi's refusal to accept political power was linked with his refusal to devise more than a tentative program for the society that might emerge from a nonviolent revolution. In accepting the power to direct others, he would be depriving them of the right to conduct their own "experiments with Truth," and in devising a rigid social structure for the future he would be denying the mutability of the quest for truth, the everlasting adjustments that in a living society would arise in response to changing human situations.

If he differed from other revolutionaries, with the exception of some anarchists, in his attitude toward power and toward the planned state of the Marxists,

Gandhi also differed from them in his attitude to Western civilization, whose mechanism and materialism he denounced as early as 1909 in his book *Hind Swaraj*. Whether of the generation of Mao Tse-tung and Ho Chi Minh who led the colonial revolutionary movements to success after World War II, or of the later generation of Third World insurrectionists typified by Che Guevara and Frantz Fanon, almost all the great anti-imperialists, with the exception of such Gandhian disciples as Vinoba Bhave and Jayaprakash Narayan, reached an ambivalent attitude toward the West. They rejected Western political and economic domination; at the same time they rejected the traditional ways of life of their own peoples and especially the religious elements that provided the foundation for the ancient cultures of Asia and Africa, replacing them by Western political forms and by Western technologies. The tragic paradox of recent Chinese history is that an external defiance of the West has been accomplished through an internal surrender to Western methods; a similar progression has occurred under revolutionary governments in other countries that have been liberated from imperialist domination.

India has been a partial exception to this kind of surrender to the West. The upper classes, the great cities, the military and administrative services are Westernized. Yet among the masses of the people this process has been slowed down by multiple forces of resistance: the deep conservatism of the peasants, the resilient pluralism of Hinduism, and, not least, the surviving influence of Gandhi, who, alone among the colonial revolutionaries, went to the West and returned unconverted. For though Gandhi learned much in the years he spent outside India, and counted Ruskin, Tolstoi, and

Thoreau among the masters who shaped his outlook, he chose no more than was needed to vitalize his own beliefs, and returned to find again, with the help of Western insights, the resources of his own tradition, out of which he drew the strength that made him so responsive to the aspirations of the Indian poor and so imaginative as a leader in the fight for liberation.

Yet, even if the strategy Gandhi evolved was fed by Indian traditions and adapted constantly to Indian circumstances, it was never exclusively Asian. Gandhi was a political as well as a religious pluralist; if he sought a faith that Christians could accept as easily as Hindus, he also sought a political method that would be universal in its applications, and it was his lack of either religious or national exclusivism that bred him enemies among chauvinists and xenophobes and led to his death. At the height of his struggle with the British, he never lost his admiration for English thinkers and English institutions, and he refused to sever the channels of dialogue with those against whom he fought without bitterness and without envy. The dialogue was successful; Gandhi's greatest achievement was that virtual conversion of the British which gradually and imperceptibly weakened to the vanishing point their will to rule as imperialists.

Later events, and especially the American civil-disobedience movement of the early 1960s, have demonstrated that the methods of nonviolent struggle advocated and developed by Gandhi are appropriate to no single time and place; they can be used as effectively in a modern technological society as in a world, like the India of the 1930s, that was barely emerging from the medievalism of the Mogul Empire. If a viable alternative to the mystiques of violence that have recently characterized radical movements in the West and in the Third

World alike is to be devised, there are few directions of search likely to be profitable; one of them is a continuation into changed times and circumstances of Gandhi's "experiments with Truth." The virtue and the meaning of those experiments were conferred by their relation to existence; they become most significant when they are considered in relation to the life in which Gandhi developed and realized them in action. It is with this interplay of the action and the idea that the rest of this book will be concerned.

ii

Even today the district of Gujarat known as Kathiawar is a remote, rarely visited part of India, separated by the great salt marshes of the Rann of Cutch to the northwest, by the ocean and the Gulf of Cambay to the south and east, and by the mountainous desert of Rajasthan to the northeast. The last Indian lions survive there, and in the hills glitter the sacred marble cities of the Jains. When Mohandas Kamarchand Gandhi was born in the seacoast town of Porbandar on October 2, 1869, Kathiawar was a maze of small principalities; more than two hundred of them, ranging in size from a few acres to hundreds of square miles, were crowded in the peninsula. They comprised in number more than a third of the native states of India, and every one of their rulers had the power of life and death over his subjects and maintained the establishment of a miniature sovereign state.

Gandhi's father, Kamarchand Gandhi, was the Prime Minister of Porbandar. The Gandhis were merchants by caste, and Banias by subcaste; their name signified "grocer," but for generations the leading members of the family had flourished in the petty politics of Kathiawar, serving as high officials in various of its larger states. In their religious connections they mirrored the unusual mixture of creeds and cultures, Jain and Hindu and Moslem, to be found in this remote corner of India—the assembled relics of long-past sea voyages by Arab traders and of flights into exile of those who feared the Mogul rulers of Delhi.

Both Kamarchand and his wife Putlibai were devout followers of the cult of Vishnu, but Putlibai came of a small sect known as the Pranamis, which mingled Hindu and Moslem beliefs to such an extent that in its temples, devoid of idols, the Koran and the sacred books of the Vaishnavites were given equal honor. Peace and good will between members of all cults were tenets of the Pranamis, as were simplicity of living, which involved strict vegetarianism, the avoidance of alcohol and tobacco, and periodic fasts. Thus, in the earliest days of his life, appeared the influences that would ultimately lead Gandhi to seek his truths in all religions and to find in the denial of the body the disciplines he needed to strengthen the will.

As well as the Pranamis, there were the Jains, who were numerous and respected in Kathiawar, and who associated freely with the local Vaishnavites. Many of the friends of Kamarchand Gandhi, and some of his spiritual advisers, were Jains, and in their company Gandhi heard for the first time as a child of the concept of ahimsa, which the Jains claimed had been originated two thousand five hundred years ago by their founder Mahavira. In fact the doctrine of ahimsa is common to Buddhism and Hinduism as well as Jainism, and it may well have developed before the three religions drew apart. *Himsa* means harm; *ahimsa* is the not-doing of harm to other beings. Certainly, whoever originated the concept, it was the Jains who most thoroughly developed it. Mahavira interpreted ahimsa's renunciation of violence as embracing not only human beings and animals, but also earth, water, fire, and wind, which he regarded as living beings and which he exhorted his followers to disturb as little as possible. "He who lights a fire," it is said in the Jain scriptures, "kills living beings; he who extinguishes it, kills the fire. Therefore a wise man who considers the law should light no fire." Porbandar was a world where such statements were heard with reverence and where Jain monks masked their mouths to avoid breathing in microscopic creatures.

Yet it was without much conscious awarenesss that Gandhi absorbed these vital early influences. He paid so little attention to them, in fact, that he did not even learn in the original the great scripture that his mother knew and loved, the Bhagavad Gita; it was in England and in English, many years later, that he discovered the poem and recognized the appropriateness to his own outlook of its injunction to live in action without regard for action's fruits.

Gandhi was a dull and timid boy, a typical late developer into genius, passing without distinction through the schools in Rajkot, where his father had become Prime Minister. Betrothed three times in childhood (twice without his knowledge), he was married at thirteen to Kasturbai, a girl of his own age, and lived in a dream of sensuality until one night, when he had hastened from his sick father to his girl-wife's bed, Kamarchand died in his absence. The memory of that desertion haunted Gandhi, made him a devoted enemy of child marriage, and twisted into revulsion the obsession with sex which he retained to the end of his life.

Kamarchand Gandhi had always hoped that one of his sons would follow him in the profession of Prime Minister; his choice had fallen on Mohandas. But the younger Gandhi's scholastic record had continued so dismally that there seemed little chance of his getting a degree even in an Indian university. He had scraped through his matriculation, but his single term at Samaldar College had been a complete failure. The family concluded that the only possible chance for such a dunce lay in going to London and keeping terms at the Inner Temple, where the examinations were reputed to be easy enough for even the dullest of students to pass.

Gandhi saw the prospect of a time in England with mingled apprehension and delight. Compared with the inhabitants of the cities of British India, the people of the native states saw little of the English, and hence were inclined to give them heroic images. Gandhi had encountered Englishmen only in the awesome capacity of school inspectors and of residents who wielded mysterious powers in the affairs of Porbandar and Rajkot and made life difficult for his father the Prime Minister. As an Indian boy in a time of rising patriotism he resented their presence in his country, yet he also admired and envied them, especially for their stature and their vigor. Taking seriously the rhyme of the Gujarati poet, Narmad:

Behold the mighty Englishman.
He rules the Indian small
Because being a meat-eater
He is five cubits tall . . .

he even allowed a Moslem schoolmate to tempt him into breaking his Vaishnava rules and taking part in secret feasts where he ate goat's meat and baker's bread. The lapse from vegetarianism ended quickly and for ever, but the fascination of the English remained (as it still haunts and influences many an Indian even a quarter of a century after Independence). The strength of Gandhi's desire to make the great journey to their home-land was tested when, having received his mother's reluctant consent, he answered the summons of the elders of his subcaste, the Modh Banias. No Modh Bania had ever crossed the dark waters, and if Gandhi did so, the elders warned him, he would be excom-municated and every caste brother would be forbidden to associate with him or assist him. Gandhi chose to be excommunicated. It was his first refusal to submit to an irrational display of authority. In September 1888, at the age of nineteen, having recently become a father, he set sail from Bombay with a trunkful of Indian sweetmeats, which formed his principal food on the voyage; the condition on which his mother had con-sented to the journey was that he take a vow not to imitate the Englishmen by eating meat.

In almost everything else he did imitate them, with a thoroughness he was later to turn to very different ends. An ironic novelist of Indian background—a Narayan or a Naipaul—would be needed to do justice to the pathetic record of Gandhi's early days in England. Arriving at the Victoria Hotel on a late autumn day in a white flannel suit, he set out with comic earnestness to become the Compleat Englishman. He bought in Bond Street a ten-guinea morning suit, and a top hat that cost nineteen shillings, and a silver-headed cane. He took lessons in elocution and dancing, in French and violin playing. He sang the hit songs and became perilously though not irrevocably involved with designing women (whom he had neglected to tell he was already married). This period of astonishing his friends by playing fashion's ape came to an end as his money ran short and his good sense prevailed; selling his violin and dismissing his teachers, he began to seek the more serious elements in English life. He found, surprisingly, that they opened to him for the first time the riches of the Indian heritage that had meant nothing to him at home in Kathiawar.

It was the one thread of Indianism he kept inviolate that led him toward the English minority of radicals and reformers among whom he could feel at home and from whom he could learn. Whatever the temptations he encountered, and however far he ingenuously succumbed to them, he never broke his vow to his mother, Putlibai, and in his early days in London he endured much embarrassment and even a little hunger by consistently refusing to eat meat. His difficulties ended when, walking by chance along Farringdon Street, he discovered a vegetarian restaurant. At the same moment he was given the key that set in motion the dialectic of idea and action he was to pursue for the rest of his life.

There was a display of literature in the restaurant. One of the books was *A Plea for Vegetarianism* by H. S. Salt, a friend of Bernard Shaw and Edward Carpenter and something of a Godwinian anarchist. Salt's book was a revelation to Gandhi, for it defended in rational terms the teachings transmitted to his half-attentive mind in childhood by means of myth and precept. The dietary exercises he began under Salt's inspiration were the first of his "experiments with Truth," the beginning of that reasoned discipline of action that would culminate in the Spartan way of life (Spartan in all but violence) of the dedicated *Satyagrahi*. He met Salt, and with his encouragement became active in vegetarian societies, his first public work. He was still so excruciatingly shy that at meetings he would ask others to read the papers and the motions he wished to present.

"One of the most significant facts about the life and vocation of Gandhi," Thomas Merton pointed out in his essay "Gandhi and the One-Eyed Giant," "was his discovery of the East through the West." It was a discovery that in a way he shared with the whole of India, for by the initiative of European scholars in the nineteenth century, ancient Indian history was re-created, the serious study of Sanskrit literature was begun, and the Indian vernaculars were treated seriously and became literary languages. Perhaps, indeed, the greatest gift the British gave to India was her past, which before they came had been lost in the pseudo-history of the Brahmins. In Gandhi's case the gift was dramatically direct. He went to England looking for the knowledge that made Englishmen powerful. He learned instead his first lessons in the knowledge that had once made Asians wise.

Toward the end of his second year in London he came into contact with the Theosophists. The books of their prophetess, Madame Blavatsky, made only a fleeting impression on him, but her followers led him to read for the first time the Indian classic he was later to regard as "the book *par excellence* for the knowledge of Truth."

This was the Bhagavad Gita, in the English translation by Sir Edwin Arnold. Later Gandhi was to make his own translation of the Gita, from the original Sanskrit into Gujarati. Arguing that the great battle of Kurukshetra, on whose eve Krishna spoke the discourse embodied in the Gita, was completely unhistorical, he presented the case—accepted by no academic Indologist and fiercely disputed by Indian patriots who believed in liberation by violence—that the whole of the Mahabharata was to be interpreted allegorically as the account of a spiritual struggle, and that when he spoke to Arjuna in the embedded Gita, Krishna did not intend to exhort a Kshatriya to do his military duty, but to teach all men the value of nonattachment and the need to act without the desire for the fruits of action.

Gandhi went on to read Arnold's long poem *The Light of Asia*, where he learned for the first time of the life and teachings of the Buddha. Then he began to study the Bible. He found the Old Testament distasteful, but the New Testament moved him deeply. At the same time he read Carlyle on Mohammed, and admired the Prophet's austere way of life. He began, tentatively, to synthesize in his mind the teachings of Christianity and Buddhism, of Islam and Vaishnavite Hinduism, and found the unifying principle in the idea of renunciation. There was a special appeal, whose implications he was to spend a lifetime working out, in the injunction of the Sermon on the Mount: "But I say unto you, that ye resist not evil." So strongly did he feel the appeal of the Christian ethic at this time that, as he admitted many years later, he wavered for a time between Christianity and Hinduism. "When I recovered my balance of mind, I felt that to me salvation was possible only through the

Hindu religion and my faith in Hinduism grew deeper and more enlightened." But it was a Hinduism that had been touched by the egalitarian implications of Christianity. As Erik Erikson remarked in his psychobiography, *Gandhi's Truth*, "He left England an augmented Indian." He was called to the bar in 1891, and almost immediately afterward sailed home to Bombay.

The three years in London had been important but not completely decisive in Gandhi's intellectual development. If in England he encountered the Asian texts that were to be most important as guides in his development of a philosophy of action—the Gita and the Sermon on the Mount—it was later, when he was working among Indians in South Africa but still partly in an English atmosphere, that he encountered the Western writers who strengthened his ideas of nonviolent action and provided a constructive basis for his theory of social reconstruction.

The first was Tolstoi, whose *The Kingdom of God Is Within You* he read in 1893. Tolstoi preached eloquently the doctrine of nonviolence, but hardly practiced it at all, and in his hands and those of his followers his pacifist anarchism remained a largely untried and therefore undeveloped doctrine. It was Gandhi who put into action what Tolstoi advocated in words. And it was Gandhi also, far more than the author himself, who found a practical application for the teachings John Ruskin developed in *Unto This Last*, which Gandhi read in 1904 and which, as he remarked, "captured me and made me transform my life."

If Tolstoi became a guide to Gandhi in developing the theory and practice of nonviolent action that he later called *Satyagraha*, it was Ruskin who led him to the conclusion that an unequal social order, divorced from the realities of labor, is likely to make nonviolence impossible. In later years, when Gandhi listed the three men who had most influenced him, the Westerners Tolstoi and Ruskin were among them; the third was a Gujarati jeweler, a contemplative Vaishnavite philosopher named Raychandbai who was the nearest Gandhi ever had to a guru in the Indian sense, and who would certainly have lived and died in obscurity if Gandhi had never known him. Another writer toward whom Gandhi felt drawn almost as strongly as toward Tolstoi and Ruskin was Henry David Thoreau, but he did not include him among the prime influences on his way of thought, and, indeed, his debt to Thoreau's *Civil Disobedience* has been much exaggerated, for it was not until Gandhi had himself started a full-scale civil-disobedience movement that he read the essay in a South African prison in 1907 and recognized in its author a precursor.

Even the influence of Tolstoi and Ruskin can be exaggerated, and Gandhi himself was inclined to do so, partly from a principle of humility that made him reluctant to accept all the credit for his achievements. He had absorbed the general idea of nonresistance before he read Tolstoi, and Tolstoi with his passionate reasoning merely strengthened the concept into a conviction. As for Ruskin, Gandhi read much more into *Unto This Last* than the author stated explicitly, when he summarized in *My Experiments with Truth* what its teachings had meant to him.

1. That the good of the individual is contained in the good of all.

2. That a lawyer's work has the same value as the barber's inasmuch as all have the same right of earning their livelihood for their work.

3. That a life of labour, i.e. the life of the tiller of the soil and the handicraftsman, is the life worth living.

Only the first of these ideas is stated clearly in *Unto This Last*. The others are, at best, implied. But by the time Gandhi encountered Ruskin's book he was ready for the message he thought he found in *Unto This Last*; he had now begun to realize that the life of a prosperous lawyer, as he had become by 1904, was incompatible with the vocation of a dedicated nonviolent revolutionary. Ruskin's importance was that he justified Gandhi in giving practical expression to the urges that were propelling him toward the life style of his later years, when manual toil would fill the gaps in a life of political activism and of communitarian existence with his followers, in settlements that combined Western hygiene, order, and efficiency with the dietary habits, household arrangements, and religious practices of Asia.

Gandhi was not in fact a widely read man, which partly explains why the minor works of Tolstoi and Ruskin assumed such importance for him. All the books that did influence him he read in the first half of his life, and he took from them only a few general ideas, which he spent the rest of his life elaborating in action. Similarly, when one reads his own writings, it is a few pungent maxims, a few bold concepts that stand out in a pattern of endless repetitions and variations on limited themes—the work of a man writing simply for simple readers in the flow of a busy existence. If Gandhi had not achieved what he did, there would be little purpose in reading him; his writings were the glosses on a life of struggle.

Shortly after his return from the West that life began to take its special shape from the conjunction of circumstances in India and South Africa and from Gandhi's awakening consciousness of the role that Providence—he was convinced—had prepared for him.

iii

Neither national liberation nor social revolution is a category sufficiently wide to contain the objective that evolved with and out of Gandhi's life of action. He was not concerned primarily with the creation of an Indian nation or with the abolition of poverty. Indeed, he was opposed to nationalism in its narrower definition, for he sought to make his fellow countrymen feel that in becoming fully Indian they were also becoming citizens of the world, unbound by exclusive loyalties of race or creed or class. And, far from wishing that men should cease to be poor, he taught that a deliberate poverty, based on the conscious shedding of attachment to material things, was the happiest of possible human conditions.

All his struggles, however various their immediate aims, were concerned fundamentally with the quality of living. He sought to make men free, and freedom implied living according to the particular way of life—religious or national—they chose. But freedom and dignity implied a respect for the freedom and dignity of others, so that in the final analysis Gandhi was more a universalist than a nationalist.

But the universal is often the complement of the intensely particular or personal, and in Gandhi's case his public actions were always related to the simple personal goal toward which he saw the life of service guiding him. It was the goal of moksha, the direct knowledge of God, the cessation of the cycle of rebirths. As the karma yogin he had chosen (or God—as he sometimes said—had led him into) the way of deeds as the path toward enlightenment, and it is possible, as it is with all the saints, to see that life of dedication, and all those complicated "experiments with Truth," as in the end a gigantic sacrifice to the self. Dying to the self is, in practice, an ego-dominated process, and it would not be wholly unjust to represent Gandhi's life as a great drama in which, audience and cast, he manipulated events to keep himself forever in the center of the stage of renunciation. For a stage it was; there was little private in the last fifty-five years of Gandhi's life. On his famous marches, in his ashrams, in the untouchables' huts and the millionaires' mansions where he periodically roosted, his life was lived in the open, and the whole world was a great joint family with no walls between him and it. He utilized the Indian love of darshan—the blessing conveyed by the mere sight of a Mahatma—to attract audiences, and he utilized the printing press to make the world his confessor in matters large and small, from his inmost spiritual longings to the life of the bed and the latrine. Incessantly he revealed himself, in action, speech, print, even, at the end, on the airwaves, and as incessantly his inmost self eluded one and perhaps eluded him. One can only speculate on the way—had he been born half a century later—he might have used television for the ironic rigors of his tantalizing candor.

When one admits in Gandhi this element of sub-limated self-absorption, and realizes that in his fervor for the Bhagavad Gita he identified himself imagina-tively with Arjuna, the purest of Indian mythical heroes (as in childhood he had identified himself with Harish-chandra, the truthful prince), it immediately appears appropriate that the two crucial episodes in determining his entry into a course of activist rebellion should have been incidents in his young manhood in which, as vic-tim, he was the central figure and in which the central issue was the assault on human dignity. Gandhi was awakened to the nature of his destiny by situations that threatened the quality of his own life; afterward he devoted himself to defending the quality of the life of others.

On his return to India in 1891 he found his personal world disintegrating at the center. His mother had died, and in Kathiawar it was obvious that the influence of the Gandhis had vanished with his father's death. There was no place for him in the princely courts of Rajkot and Porbandar, and the little towns of the peninsula had already a surplus of practicing lawyers. Gandhi there-fore decided to practice in Bombay, but his career there came to a quick and humiliating end; the barrister of the Inner Temple, rising to address the court for the first time, was struck dumb with stage fright and had to withdraw from his case. Defeated, he went back to Rajkot and managed to sustain the household he was trying desperately to Anglicize (with knives and forks and meals at table) by earning a few rupees writing petitions and memoranda to present to the local native courts.

He had left England with good memories of the country and its people and—like so many educated nineteenth-century Indians—with a genuine reverence for the liberal philosophies and democratic institutions Britain had created. His scanty contact with the British in India had not prepared him for the differences that may appear between men when they live at ease in their own country, and the same men when they live abroad under the tensions that beset those who rule over an alien people. Now he was to learn that difference to his own discomfort.

In England, at one of the houses he visited, he had met a certain Charles Ollivant, a polite and apparently friendly fellow guest with whom he had enjoyed long and cordial conversations. Ollivant was by profession a civil servant in India, and on returning from leave he was appointed resident in Porbandar. When Gandhi's elder brother was accused of some obscure palace intrigue in his capacity of secretary to the Rana of Porbandar, traditions of family solidarity demanded that Gandhi should call on Ollivant and plead the brother's case. Against his better judgment Gandhi went, to be received coldly and told that his brother must state his complaints through the usual official channels. When he tried to argue, he was told to leave, and eventually was forcibly removed by the resident's peon. He protested in writing; it was an affront to his dignity. The resident sent a reply that suggested that an Indian might have no dignity to defend. When the celebrated Parsi advocate Sir Pherozeshah Mehta arrived in Rajkot, Gandhi asked his advice. Mehta remarked loftily that the young lawyer evidently did not know the British, and that if he wanted to earn a living in Kathiawar he must quietly pocket the insult. "Tell him he has yet to know life."

"The advice was bitter poison to me," Gandhi remembered, "but I had to accept it. . . . This shock changed the course of my life."

He gained from the incident a first insight into how human relationships may be corrupted when one people rules another; only later was he to realize that the same corruption was rotting the Indian community itself as a result of the discriminations created by the caste system. He knew that his living in Kathiawar could only be earned at courts under Ollivant's surveillance, and he knew also that to continue would involve intolerable humiliations. He must find a living elsewhere. The opportunity presented itself unexpectedly when one of the Moslem trading houses of Porbandar invited him to assist them in South Africa in a case that involved another merchant from Kathiawar. They had engaged European lawyers, but they would be happier if an Indian were also there to offer advice. Gandhi accepted at once. It was a vague assignment, and when he sailed from Bombay in April 1893 he had no idea of his precise duties in Durban and certainly no premonition that he had made the crucial decision of his life.

Gandhi received his first lesson on the position of Indians in South Africa when he entered the courtroom in Durban wearing a black turban with his frock coat. The magistrate ordered him to remove it; Gandhi politely refused and walked out of the court; he also wrote to the newspaper explaining his act. This attracted the attention of both the Europeans, some of whom wrote angry replies, and the Indians, who regarded with a certain pitying surprise this young newcomer who had obviously not appreciated the peculiar position of his people in South Africa.

Indians in India might be ruled arbitrarily by their British overlords, but at least they were in their own country and the British were a tiny minority. In South Africa it was the Indians who were an alien minority, and a minority without power. In the 1890s there were over two million Africans and about three-quarters of a million Europeans in the British colonies of Natal and Cape Colony and the autonomous Boer territories of Transvaal and the Orange Free State. There were altogether about seventy-five thousand Indians, less than three per cent of the total population of South Africa. The first had come in the early 1860s to Natal, mainly from the Madras area of India, to work as indentured laborers in the sugar plantations. This was virtual serfdom, but at least it was terminable, and after five years the laborer might remain as a free man. Those who stayed were often joined by their womenfolk, and a kind of Indian aristocracy arrived consisting of Moslem merchants and Parsi clerks. Because of the illiteracy and primitive habits of the Tamil laborers, Hindus were despised and called Sammys, a corruption of the Tamil word *swami*, which actually means master; in South Africa it took on the connotation of coolie, and the Moslems and Parsis sought to evade the stigma by evoking their ancestries and calling themselves Arabs and Persians respectively. By wearing a Hindu turban, Gandhi had placed himself in the despised class of the Sammys, for few white South Africans cared to distinguish between a plantation coolie and an educated Indian barrister.

His situation was to be emphasized dramatically by a series of incidents that in retrospect Gandhi came to regard as marking the point in life when the strength of his feelings shifted the compass of his thought for ever and made his later career inevitable. To represent the interests of his employer, Dada Abdulla, he had to travel to Pretoria, and at Durban he entered a first-class compartment with a first-class ticket. The train climbed up from the coast into the mountains and at night stopped at Pietermaritzburg, the capital of Natal. A white passenger entered the compartment, looked at Gandhi, went away, and returned with a railway official, who ordered Gandhi to the luggage van. Gandhi refused, and was ejected from the train. He spent the night shivering in the station waiting room. The next day he traveled on without difficulty to the railhead at Charlestown, but on the stagecoach that carried him to Johannesburg the nightmare of discrimination was repeated, for the guard of the coach first refused to let him travel inside and then tried to force him to sit on a mat at the driver's feet. When Gandhi protested, the man attempted to drag him off the coach, and then beat him until the passengers intervened. On the last stage of the journey, when he took the train from Johannesburg to Pretoria, a guard again tried to force him out of a first-class carriage, but this time an English passenger took his part and he was allowed to stay. Even this kindness only emphasized the lesson that in South Africa Indians had no real rights; whatever liberties they enjoyed were at the whim of the whites who ruled the country. In one way they were even worse off than the Negroes, who at least did not live under the threat of deportation.

This, as Gandhi discovered, was a threat becoming

daily more urgent so far as the Indians were concerned. White merchants found the thrifty Indian traders dangerous competitors, and the Boers were opposed to them because of their color. In Transvaal and the Orange Free State they were not allowed to vote, and in Pretoria they were subjected to a curfew. In Natal they still enjoyed civil rights as British subjects, but there were agitations on foot to disenfranchise them as soon as Natal became a self-governing colony, and the more extreme xenophobes talked of the deportation of Indian laborers or at least of heavy discriminatory taxes.

Spurred by his own experiences, Gandhi called the Indians of Pretoria to a meeting where, losing the shyness that up to this point had kept him in obscurity, he took advantage of his education and profession to assert —at twenty-three—his power of leadership. He exhorted the Indians to change their habits so that the Europeans could no longer accuse them of filthiness, to learn English so as to integrate more easily into the community, to defend their rights. Thus, from the start, he linked the idea of self-improvement with the struggle to win one's rights from others. He himself began, not unexpectedly, by trying to force the railway to end discrimination; his efforts bore fruit in the autumn of 1893 when an Indian successfully sued the company after he had been ejected from a train.

The agitation might have ended with this token triumph, for Gandhi settled, by arbitration that saved faces on both sides, the case that had brought him to South Africa, and in April 1894, his passage booked to Bombay, he sat down to a farewell dinner organized by Dada Abdulla. At the table he picked up a newspaper and saw a headline: "Indian Franchise Bill." The legislators of Natal were hastening to use their newly acquired power of self-government to restrict the number of the self-governed by taking the vote away from the Indians. Gandhi turned the dinner into a political meeting and before it ended a committee had been formed, funds subscribed, and Gandhi persuaded to stay and lead the fight.

He found himself at the head of a miniature mass movement dedicated to peaceful agitation. In imitation of the Indian National Congress which Alan Octavius Hume had called together in 1885 (and which had not yet adopted the objective of Indian independence), he founded the Natal Indian Congress, and organized petitions to the Natal legislature and later to the British Colonial Office. As so often in later life, he had to be content with partial successes. Indians already on the voting list were allowed to remain there, but no new Indian names would be added. A proposed annual tax on indentured laborers of twenty-five pounds (more than their actual earnings) was reduced to three. The extent of discrimination was narrowed; the fact remained.

Gandhi did not give up the struggle. In fact, he was to stay in South Africa, with brief intervals abroad, until 1914, and during that time his principal concern was the liberation of the Indian community in South Africa. (Parenthetically one may observe that his concern for the rights of the native people does not appear to have gone beyond expressions of compassion during the Zulu rebellion of 1906.) These twenty years, when he was forging the weapons of struggle he later used in India for the liberation of a nation rather than a minority, fall into two clearly defined periods. In the first Gandhi pursues the career of a prospering Anglophile lawyer and leads a movement dedicated to agitation through legal channels. In the second, beginning in

1904 after his reading of *Unto This Last*, he completely changes his life style, takes to simplified communal living, accepts the ascetic discipline of brahmacharya, or complete chastity, and turns from legal agitation to nonviolent campaigns of open lawbreaking, which he wages under the banner of *Satyagraha*, or truth-force.

The earlier period was not without heroic passages. Returning from India in 1896 with his family, he found himself execrated in Durban for remarks that Reuters had misquoted. He always maintained that cowardice was worse even than violence, and on this occasion, against the advice of his friends, he insisted on walking off the ship in broad daylight; he might have been killed by the mob if the wife of the police superintendent of Durban had not spiritedly intervened and fenced them off with her umbrella. Gandhi's Tolstoyism made him refuse to prosecute his assailants, and he later regarded the incident as a useful test of his power to accept evil without retaliation.

He continued, during this first period, to use the Natal Congress as an instrument of legal agitation against discriminatory legislation but without great success. He did so in the name of British democratic concepts, since he still believed that the British Empire was disinterestedly concerned for the peoples it ruled, and that what was happening in South Africa was merely a localized aberration that would eventually be corrected. "I then believed," he afterward recalled, "that the British Empire existed for the welfare of the world. A genuine loyalty prevented me from even wishing ill of the Empire."

This faith in the good will inspiring British imperialism explains why, in the Boer War, Gandhi organized an Indian Ambulance Corps of eleven hundred men, repeating the action during the Zulu uprising of 1906 (when he accepted the rank of sergeant-major) and again in London during 1914, when he raised a third Indian contingent, which he was too ill to join. The militant nationalists in India criticized these actions, but Gandhi's justifications were not without logic.

He did not even begin to contemplate complete separation of India or the Indians from the Empire until, during World War I, he was finally convinced that it was not possible for justice to be done to the colonial peoples under British rule. And there were matters of principle involved. Gandhi believed that one was only justified in resisting a war if one had made clear statements of opposition beforehand; this was an example of his concept of frank and open politics. Further, he argued that, if one were fighting for rights as a British subject, as the Indians were doing in South Africa, one tacitly assumed a duty to help defend the Empire one hoped would guarantee such rights. Finally, he extended an argument that curiously anticipated George Orwell's polemics against the pacifists of Britain during World War II: those who accept the protection of the British Navy have no right to deny their help to an embattled Britain, especially when that help can be given in a nonviolent way by rendering aid to suffering human beings.

In retrospect, the most important aspect of these military interludes in Gandhi's career is the scale of priorities they suggest. The two basic elements in the Gandhian social philosophy were established before their originator became even in his own special way an Indian nationalist. Between 1904 and 1908 he sketched in theory and in practice his doctrine of *Satyagraha* and of the constructive reordering of society on the basis of simplified communitarian living. At this stage, if it had been possible for Indians in South Africa and India to gain full civil rights under British rule, he would not have insisted on a change in the titular superstructure, which was largely irrelevant to his goal of changing the quality of individual and social life. He became a nationalist only reluctantly, partially, and as a last resort; and the creation of a formally independent India was always secondary, in his calculations, to transformations on other levels than the political that he considered necessary for a life that would be at the same time free and, in his sense, religious. In this direction he differed emphatically from the real Indian nationalists, whether they were Hindu traditionalists like Tilak or LSE socialists like Nehru, and the fragility of his alliance with them was eventually to be shown when he accepted in 1947 the fact that the actual liberation of India was not the kind of liberation he had been seeking.

So much good will among white South Africans seemed to be generated by the record of the Indian Ambulance Corps during the Boer War that the Natal Congress assumed it was only a matter of time before justice would be done to the Indian claims, and in 1901 Gandhi left for India, where the leader of the moderate wing in Congress, Gopal Krishna Gokhale, believed there was an important role for him to play in gaining home rule for his country. Once again Gandhi started a lawyer's practice in Bombay, but early in 1902 a cable arrived from Durban calling on him to redeem a pledge he had given to return if he were needed. Contrary to expectations, the British victory had not brought an improvement in the prospects of the Indians; the government in Whitehall was mainly anxious to promote a reconciliation between British and Boers, and the other races were disregarded in the drive for white unity.

Gandhi set up a law office in Johannesburg to defend Indian rights through the courts, and in 1904 established the first of his many newspapers, *Indian Opinion*, as a means of educating and consolidating the community. In 1904, responding to the light which he felt *Unto This Last* had ignited in his mind, he established outside Johannesburg a community called Phoenix Farm, and there he ruled as patriarch over a joint family of Indians and sympathetic European vegetarians while still pursuing his legal career. The shift to community living was only the first in a series of changes in his way of life prompted by a developing sense of religious dedication. In 1906, on night marches during the Zulu campaign, he decided to abandon the desire for children and wealth and take the way of brahmacharya. Sexual desire, he decided, could cloud the spirit, and therefore physical intercourse should take place only for procreation. Many years later the hope that the people of India would be taught the wisdom of self-restraint made him reject birth control as a means of regulating population. Meanwhile, the abandonment of sexual relations did not appear to him a deprivation; rather, it was a liberation from a guilt that had haunted him since the night of his father's death, and he believed that it would widen the possibilities of other intimacies on the level of shared work and ideals which he tried to establish in his successive communities and ashrams. Brahmacharya was also a stage in the education in self-restraint that Gandhi came to regard as necessary for the kind of nonviolent action he had been contemplating if the Indians had to move beyond legal methods in the struggle to win their rights. The necessity for such action soon arose.

In 1906 legislation was proposed in the Transvaal that

would require the registration and fingerprinting of all Indians; it would give the police power to enter Indian houses without warrants to make sure the inhabitants were registered. Apart from the general indignity of the ordinance, the Moslems were particularly incensed by the inclusion of women, which involved a breach of purdah. Gandhi called a meeting on September 11 in the Empire Theatre at Johannesburg. The building was packed to the door by excited, angry Indians. After Gandhi had warned them what resistance might mean in terms of imprisonment and the destruction of businesses, they took by acclamation a vow to reject registration. It was characteristic of the feeling among Indians at this time that the meeting ended with cheers for King Edward and the singing of the national anthem. Westminster was still seen as the fount of justice, and Gandhi was sent there to present the Indians' view to the colonial office. The British government disallowed the legislation, but it was a shallow victory for the Indians, since at the beginning of 1907 Transvaal regained self-government and elected a Boer-dominated administration led by Generals Botha and Smuts. The registration law was passed, and on July 1 all Indians, without exception, were required to register.

To counter the law Gandhi put into operation the first *Satyagraha* movement. He had chosen the name because he did not like either *passive resistance*, a merely negative procedure that he regarded as the weapon of the weak, or *civil disobedience*, which had an aura of defiant hostility. The resistance he wished to offer would be that of people who did not fear to be violent but chose deliberately to be nonviolent and to fight by the power of truth rather than by the power of the body. It would be a resistance totally without hostility, since, as Gandhi argued:

> Man and his deed are two distinct things. Whereas a good deed should call forth approbation and a wicked deed disapprobation, the doer of the deed, whether good or wicked, always deserves respect or pity as the case may be. "Hate the sin but not the sinner" is a precept which, though easy enough to understand, is rarely practiced, and that is why the poison of hatred spreads in the world.

At the same time, *Satyagraha* would have its positive elements. It would begin with the statement of clearly limited aims and with the announcement of the tactics to be employed. It would attempt to convert the opponent (never to be regarded as the enemy) by the example of suffering willingly endured. Ideally, there should be no moral coercion, while compromise with honor was implied in the whole conception, since the desired result was a settlement in which neither side would feel itself humiliated. In this way both sides would in the end gain, since society would have become a little more just and more harmonious. Thus the power of truth would be revealed and *Satyagraha* consummated. As the theory and practice of *Satyagraha* evolved in struggle after struggle in India and South Africa, Gandhi came to regard it as a strategy that, if only its practitioners were trained in self-restraint and as willing as soldiers to die for their cause, was indefinitely flexible and could be used under any conditions and against any opponent.

The *Satyagraha* campaigns in South Africa continued intermittently and with rising intensity from the summer of 1907 to the beginning of 1914. They secured a limited victory for the Indians in South Africa, but their main interest lies in the fact that they were the first experiments in Gandhian civil resistance—the war games, as it were, by which the strategy and tactics to be used in a variety of Indian situations were developed and tested. In the history of South Africa they have turned out to be of marginal importance; in the history of India they are crucial.

The first campaign in 1907 began with the peaceful picketing of registration centers by Gandhi's volunteers, most of them teen-age boys, who had been strictly instructed not to molest or insult any Indians who wished to register. In fact only a small minority—no more than one Indian in twenty—complied with the law. After a series of warnings, the government began making arrests and heroes, and in January 1908 Gandhi's turn came. He was sentenced to two months' imprisonment, the first of many such terms, but within a few days he was spirited out of his cell to secret discussions with General Smuts. A strange compromise appears to have been reached, though there are contradictory accounts of what actually took place. According to Gandhi, Smuts conceded that if the Indians registered voluntarily, the law would be repealed; Smuts later denied any such promise. Gandhi, believing that there had been a promise, persuaded his fellow Indians that they should register, an action which resulted in the first attempt on his life, by a group of enraged Pathans who—correctly as it turned out—did not believe that the law would be repealed.

As the months went on and no repeal came, Gandhi turned to new forms of resistance. Indians were sent out to trade without licenses in the streets, so that they could be imprisoned and fill the jails. Then, in August 1908, when it became clear that Smuts had no intention of keeping his promise, a gathering of three thousand Indians burned their registration cards before the mosque in Johannesburg. Gandhi was arrested for having no registration card in October and again in the following February. He went to prison on both occasions, as did many of his followers.

In 1909, Gandhi sailed again to England in the hope of securing, in the negotiations for the unification of South Africa, some guarantee of the status of Indians. He won the support of a former Viceroy of India, Lord Ampthill, but the British government was unwilling to put pressure on Smuts and Botha, and Gandhi returned to South Africa to find that the authorities were replying to *Satyagraha* with a campaign of varied harassment. He arrived just in time to prevent, through court action, a mass deportation of Indians from Durban.

Two years of stalemate followed. *Satyagraha* had made registration unenforceable, but the Indian militants were subjected to successive cat-and-mouse imprisonments. In 1912, after the aged Gokhale had come from India to negotiate with the South African government, the registration law was finally brought to an end by the maneuver of transferring Indian affairs to the Union government; once again a promise appears to have been broken, for, after telling Gokhale that the three-pound head tax on indentured labor would be repealed, Smuts refused to keep his word. The final provocation came when the Supreme Court of South Africa ruled that Moslem, Parsi, and Hindu marriages were invalid.

Gandhi replied by widening the front of action and turning from passive to active defiance of discriminatory laws. He informed the government that he would ask the Indian mineworkers to strike if the poll tax were not repealed, and when Smuts did not reply, Gandhi showed his tactical virtuosity by mobilizing the Indian women. A contingent marched illegally over the border from Transvaal into the Natal coalfields and called out the miners. Successive waves of women followed them and were arrested, embarrassing the prison authorities with their numbers. Gandhi now summoned the miners to join him in a march into the Transvaal, which would end at Tolstoi Farm, his second community, founded in 1910. Gandhi was arrested, and the two thousand marchers were eventually herded into trains and sent to jails in Natal; two Europeans who helped Gandhi to organize the march were imprisoned. This merely provoked the rest of the miners and the indentured plantation workers to join the strike. The government resorted to violence and attacked the striking miners with whips and rifle fire.

Those rifleshots gave Gandhi the moral victory. World opinion condemned the South African authorities. The viceroy of Indian protested strongly. Gandhi, as soon as he was liberated, held a mass meeting to mourn the dead miners; as a symbolic gesture he abandoned for good the European dress he had affected since his first voyage to England, and appeared barefooted and shaven. He planned another great march. And then he delivered the nonviolent *coup-de-grâce*, for the white railway workers went on strike and Gandhi immediately canceled his march. He declared the *Satyagraha* did not allow one to take advantage of an opponent's unforeseen misfortunes. His action—which appealed to the British tradition of fair play—assured a victory that was more than moral, for Smuts was now cornered by public opinion. He had to negotiate, and the result was the passage in the summer of 1914 of the Indian Relief Act, which recognized Indian marriages, dropped the poll tax, mitigated the immigration regulations, and provided for phasing out the indentured labor system.

It was an example of how, with clearly defined aims and flexible tactics, a well-conducted civil-resistance movement could embarrass an opponent superior in numbers and physical power, and could eventually mobilize public opinion by the display of suffering stoically endured and of chivalrous generosity at the psychological moment. But there were special circumstances that contributed to Gandhi's victory in this instance. South Africa was a young dominion still insecurely struggling toward nationhood; the government was inexperienced and troubled by internal tensions between British and Boers and between European workers and their employers. And in 1914 a South African government was not in the position where it could safely flout world opinion or defy a disapproving British government. In the short run circumstances were in Gandhi's favor. In the long run it was a doubtful victory, for all the gains Gandhi won were lost in the end, and no leader rose among the Indians of South Africa after his departure who could defend their interests as the racialist policies of successive governments were enforced with progressively increased severity.

But at the time it seemed a great triumph, and in July 1914, when Gandhi finally left South Africa to return, via London, to India, his reputation as a victor went before him.

iv

To follow a philosophy that evolves in action often involves a certain manipulation of chronology, and in tracing the manner in which Gandhi developed the theory and practice of *Satyagraha* in South Africa between 1904 and 1914 I have inevitably neglected the fact that geographical distance from India did not lessen his concern for the plight of its people. His position was rather like that of an actor who is at first uncertain of his talents; he develops them on a small provincial stage, but his eyes are always on the great theater of the metropolis. In the same way, South Africa gave Gandhi the limited field in which he could overcome his initial nervousness and develop his techniques. But his success there merely heightened his sense that India was the stage on which, on a mass scale, *Satyagraha* would produce its most dramatic and revolutionary results.

Only twice between 1893 and 1914 did Gandhi revisit India. On the first occasion, in 1896, he intended to return to South Africa with his family after he had revisited Kathiawar—where characteristically he became involved in inspecting latrines during a plague scare—and had lectured in the principal Indian cities on the plight of Indians in South Africa. On this occasion he did not become involved in Indian affairs, but he did meet the two rival Congress leaders, Gokhale and Bal Gandhadhar Tilak. Gokhale was a moderate who derived his liberal ideas from the tradition of Hinduism modified by Western liberalism that had been founded in the early nineteenth century by Ram Mohun Roy and his followers in the reform movement known as Brahmo Samaj. Tilak, on the other hand, was a Hindu extremist, filled with the fire of Maratha traditions, who had emerged into prominence in 1891, when he led the traditionalists in resistance to legislation establishing a legal age of consent for Indian marriages.

These two men represented the main opposing trends that were emerging in Indian native politics as Congress evolved from the open forum of Hume's vision to an organization dedicated to voicing the demands of educated Indians, which increasingly came to regard home rule as the lowest possible demand. The main questions were (1) the extent and pace of severance from British rule and (2) the means to be adopted in gaining whatever degree of autonomy was desired. Gokhale favored gradualist, legal action; Tilak became the leader of the physical-activist group, and if he did not explicitly advocate terrorism, some of his disciples favored and eventually practiced it.

Tilak was inclined, in reaction from the Anglicizing tendencies of Indian liberals, to accept Hindu society as it was, and to argue that the loss of any part of the structure, however repugnant, could only harm the whole. Gokhale, on the other hand, was as sensitive as the Brahmo Samajists two generations before to the flaws in Indian society that Western ideas had revealed with X-ray sharpness. He admired the social gospel that Vivekananda and the Ramakrishna Order had endeavored to inject into Hinduism, and in 1905 he founded the Servants of India, a society dedicated to social work, including famine relief, the uplift of untouchables, and the organization of the urban workers into trade unions.

Gandhi respected Tilak for his intelligence and his dedication, but the two men differed profoundly in personality and in their approach to the religion that for both of them was the core of their politics. Both were dedicated to action, and both found in the Bhagavad Gita a basic textbook. Their fundamental divergences were mirrored in their differing interpretations of the poem. For if Gandhi believed that it must be understood allegorically as a tract on nonviolence, Tilak believed it must be taken literally, as an exhortation to commit violence if one's cause (*swaraj*, or self-government, in his case) demanded it.

Yet, though Gandhi felt more sympathy for Gokhale than for Tilak and became his protégé, his ideas and policies reconciled to a great extent the currents within the Indian renaissance which the two older men represented. He was at once universalist and traditionalist, and this explains his later acceptance as leader by Indians of widely differing viewpoints. He had read Western philosophers with attention, he had accepted what he found good in Christianity and Islam, he respected the ideals on which British institutions appeared to be based. Yet, though he rejected violence, he was an activist willing to resort to extra-legal means, which Gokhale was not, and his experiences in South Africa, combined with his readings of Tolstoi and Ruskin, had led him to despise the materialism and the soulless machine worship that seemed to characterize Western civilization.

As he reacted against the duplicity of South African politicians and responded to inner calls to simplify his own life by brahmacharya and communal living, Gandhi began to look back nostalgically toward India and its native way of life—the life he had once been so eager to shed. As he thought out his strategy of nonviolence, he tended to forget the influence of Tolstoi and to see it in Indian terms as a form of traditional ahimsa. This feeling, that there was something specifically Asian about *Satyagraha*, he maintained to the end of his life. "Two paths are open before India today," he said in 1921, "either to introduce the Western principle of 'Might is Right,' or to uphold the Eastern principle that truth alone conquers, that truth knows no mishap, that the strong and the weak have alike a right to secure justice."

His turning away from the West found its first emphatic expression in two documents that he composed during that frustrating trip to England in 1909 when he tried to persuade the British government to safeguard Indian rights in South Africa. One was a "Confession of Faith," which he drafted after addressing a gathering of Quakers on differences between Eastern and Western concepts of existence. The other was a pamphlet, *Hind Swaraj*, his first work presenting his views on the situation in India; Indian terrorists were active in England at this time, and he wrote the pamphlet as an imaginary dialogue between a "reader" who favored terrorism and an "editor" who was obviously the mouthpiece for Gandhi's views. In both pieces the direction of attack is cultural rather than political. When the "reader" suggests that India should free herself by a campaign of assassinations and then, like Japan, establish a modern military state, the "editor" replies, "You want British rule without the Englishman. You want the tiger's nature but not the tiger." In the "Confession of Faith" Gandhi claims that to replace British rule by "Indian rule based on modern methods" would be no improvement at all. Let the Englishmen remain in India, he argues in *Hind Swaraj*, let them rule even, so long as they do so as the servants of the people and respect Indian customs.

The important point, as he repeatedly emphasizes, is not the evil of British rule; it is the evil of "modern civilization," which has become entirely material. "It is not the British people who rule India, but modern civilization rules India through its railways, telegraph, telephone, etc." Indians must unlearn all they have learned from the West in material terms: give up machinery, modern transport, even modern medicine. They must—he makes a special point of this—give up wearing machine-made cloth whether it comes from European or Indian mills. They must reconstruct the traditional culture of India's seven hundred thousand villages, where the majority of its people live.

Gandhi was later to modify this vision in a number of ways. He came to see the need for the British to depart; he acknowledged that simple machines might have their uses without causing corruption of manners;

he never got out of the habit of using railways. But when he returned to India in 1914 it was with the thought firmly in his mind that the India of the future must be based on a revival of the village and its traditions of craftsmanship. The wearing of *khaddar*, or handspun cloth, was to become in his mind—and later in the minds of all Indians—the mark of a man who sought India's freedom, while the spinning wheel (which he had not even seen when he wrote *Hind Swaraj*) would become the very symbol of his philosophy and, eventually, incorporated in its flag, the symbol of modern India.

When Gandhi had returned to India in 1901 it had been without triumphs to his credit; the perfunctory way in which Congress that year passed his resolution on conditions in South Africa—giving him five minutes to speak—showed how insignificantly he then appeared. The most revelatory experience of that visit was not his meeting with the members of Congress, mainly middle-class lawyers, but a great third-class railway journey through most of India on which he learned for the first time the variety which his country combined with an ubiquitous poverty. His fellow Indians shocked him by their filthy habits and their ill manners, but he looked on them with compassion as the victims of an evil system.

When he returned in 1915 it was as a celebrated man, like one of those leaders of brilliant frontier campaigns who come back after years of absence with the breath of novelty and an aura of uncorrupted success. The Governor of Bombay received him, and he and his disciples from Tolstoi Farm were welcomed by the notable sage and gaseous poet, Rabindranath Tagore, at his free university of Santiniketan; not long afterward Tagore conferred on Gandhi the title of Mahatma, or Great Soul, which he wore rather like a hair shirt for the rest of his life. In May 1915 he moved to the textile-making town of Ahmedabad and established the Satyagraha Ashram, a somewhat monastic institution in which personal possessions, foreign cloth, and spicy foods were forbidden, and in which Gandhi immediately showed Indians that he meant what he said about the abuses of Hinduism by accepting untouchables as members. It was the beginning of an obstinate campaign on behalf of the outcastes that for the rest of his life was to be interwoven with his other activities.

The years immediately following Gandhi's return to India formed a kind of apprenticeship to the moral leadership of the movement for India's regeneration. The old leaders of Congress were beginning to depart. Gokhale died soon after Gandhi's return, Tilak was to die in 1920, and Annie Besant, who became president of Congress in 1917, was too moderate to retain her once considerable influence in the upsurge of discontent and militancy that followed the end of World War I.

Even though Gandhi was probably not consciously awaiting the mantle of leadership, he quickly became involved after his return to India in a series of actions that introduced him to Indians as yet hardly touched by Congress activities—to students, peasants, and industrial workers—as an activist of radical views and actions to fit them. He became a hero among students in 1916 when he offended Annie Besant and almost ruined the opening of her Hindu University at Benares by delivering a speech in which he bluntly told the Indians that they should set their own houses in order before they indulged in thoughts of getting rid of the British. He condemned their unwillingness to speak in their own vernaculars, he talked scathingly of the filth of Benares and its temples, he reproached the native princes on the dais behind him for appearing in jewelry paid for by the peasants' toil, he mocked the precautions taken for the security of the Viceroy, and he attacked the terrorists who made those precautions necessary, though at the same time he admitted the impatience that bred them. "I am myself an anarchist," he said, "but of another type." And finally, as the maharajahs began to leave the platform where such dangerous things were being said, he made the statement that defined absolutely the difference between his view of the way to fight a revolution and that of the terrorists:

If I should find it necessary for the salvation of India that the English should retire, that they should be driven out, I would not hesitate to declare that they would have to go, and I hope I would be prepared to die in the defence of that belief. That would, in my opinion, be an honourable death. The bomb-thrower creates secret plots, is afraid to come into the open, and when caught pays the penalty of misdirected zeal.

Gandhi had not yet said that the English should go, but he was telling them how he would do it, and shortly afterward he gave two striking exhibitions of the power of *Satyagraha* transferred to Indian conditions. The opportunities came to him unsought, but he made the best of them, with the result that when he came to fight the British authorities on India on a wide front after the war, he had already won notable successes against two powerful groups, the British planters and the Indian textile manufacturers, and a mild success against the local representatives of government in Bihar.

In December 1916 Gandhi attended the meeting of

Congress which that year was held in Lucknow. He played a relatively undramatic part, leaving the limelight to Tilak, Mrs. Besant, and Jinnah, who was present as a fraternal delegate of the Moslem League. The occasion was memorable in one way because he met there for the first time Jawaharlal Nehru. "All of us admired him for his heroic fight in South Africa," Nehru remembered, "but he seemed very distant and different and unpolitical to many of us young men." More immediately important than this meeting was the appearance of a peasant from a remote district of Bihar who had found his way to the meeting of Congress and by some accurate intuition had surmised that of all the thousands of delegates and visitors Gandhi was the man most likely to be of help to the farmers he represented. They were indigo growers from Champaran on the marches of Nepal, who worked under almost feudal conditions as sharecroppers for the English planters. When the indigo market declined because of the invention of aniline dyes, the planters sought to compensate themselves by demanding cash instead of indigo from the peasants; they established a reign of terror to ensure that there would be little defaulting. This situation had lasted for years, and the local lawyers had drawn profit from the peasants' attempt to obtain redress without achieving anything on their behalf.

Gandhi arrived in Bihar and gained his first triumph by recruiting the lawyers, led by Rajendra Prasad, who later became President of India, as his assistants. He entered the area of the dispute. The police ordered him to leave. He refused, was brought before the magistrate, and pleaded guilty, having already persuaded the lawyers to offer themselves for arrest as *Satyagrahis* after his departure to prison. Their cooperation was not needed. The Lieutenant-Governor of Bihar ordered that proceedings be dropped, and an inquiry was set on foot, in which Gandhi and his volunteers took the most active part, with the result that the peasants' grievances were recognized and the planters forced to refund much of the money they had extorted.

Gandhi not only saved the peasants of Champaran from exploitation. He also set on foot the first of many Gandhian village improvement projects in India, establishing schools run by volunteers, organizing drainage and clean-up projects, and providing modest clinics. Though it did not last long, owing to the unavailability at this early stage of sufficient volunteers, the scheme in Champaran was an example of the practicality of Gandhi's mind; it provided also, for Gandhi, a revelation of the depths of misery to which the Indian village in the twentieth century had descended.

To the peasants of Champaran the victory over the planters was most important. To Indians in general the sensational feature of the incident was that Gandhi had calmly defied the British government in India, and the government had backed down. It was almost a textbook example of successful *Satyagraha*: a single *Satyagrahi* had offered himself for suffering and had won without having to endure it. It seemed to bear out Gandhi's contention that one man with truth on his side could wield immense moral power.

The second example of successful *Satyagraha* was conducted within the Indian community. It was a strange contest, for Gandhi, in alliance with the sister of an Ahmedabad millowner, was leading a strike against the millowner in question, who happened also to be his friend and a benefactor of his ashram. It was a dispute over wages, related to the increased cost of living that the war had caused. The owners, led by Ambalal Sarabhai, were offering a twenty per cent increase; the workers, led by Anasuya Sarabhai, wanted thirty-five per cent. Gandhi agreed to lead them if they accepted his conditions:

1. never to resort to violence,
2. never to molest blacklegs,
3. never to depend on alms, and
4. to remain firm, no matter how long the strike continued, and to earn bread, during the strike, by any honest labour.

Gandhi's theory of strikes differed from the normal one in that he did not regard them as weapons of economic coercion. To him they were the extension of *Satyagraha* into the industrial field—aimed at persuading the employer through the example of suffering for truth.

For two weeks the strike continued with no weakening on either side. Then the resolve of the workers began to surrender to their hunger. Suddenly, at a strike meeting, "the light came" to Gandhi, and he announced that unless the strikers rallied and fought to the end he would cease to eat. It was the first time he had used the fast as a weapon of *Satyagraha* (though he had once gone into a penitential fast when two boys at Tolstoi Farm were caught in sodomy), and a powerful one it proved, for the millowners immediately agreed to negotiate, and in what Gandhi insisted should be a compromise solution so as to leave no hard feelings, the strike was settled; finally, by arbitration, the strikers gained all they had asked. The indirect results of the strike were more lasting than those of the *Satyagraha* at Champaran, for it led to the foundation of the one Gandhian trade union, the Ahmedabad Textile Labor

Association; this still thrives in the 1970s as a workers' organization that by a skillful use of arbitration has secured wages and conditions of employment unequaled elsewhere in India's textile factories, and that carries on a wide variety of mutual-aid activities among the workers.

The use of the fast in the Ahmedabad strike confronts one with an equivocal feature of *Satyagraha* and, indeed, of all related civil-disobedience methods. Gandhi declared that true *Satyagraha* should not seek even the moral coercion of the opponent; it should aim at his entirely voluntary surrender to the *Satyagrahi's* point of view. Yet there is no doubt that the fast at Ahmedabad did in fact result in an act of coercion, and of this Gandhi was uncomfortably aware.

> My fast was not free from a grave defect [he said afterward] . . . I enjoyed very close and cordial relations with the mill-owners and my fast could not but affect their decision. As a Satyagrahi I knew that I might not fast against them, but ought to leave them free to be influenced by the millhands' strike alone. My fast was undertaken not on account of a lapse of the mill-owners, but on account of that of the labourers in which, as their representative, I felt I had a share. With the mill-owners, I could only plead; to fast against them would amount to coercion. Yet in spite of my knowledge that my fast was bound to put pressure on them, as in fact it did, I felt I could not help it. The duty to undertake it seemed to me to be clear.

There would be many other occasions in Gandhi's life when he would see just as clearly the duty to perform fasts that were equally dramatic, equally effective, and equally coercive. On such occasions one feels that

Gandhi's sense of the symbolic, his intuitive knowledge of the right act and the right moment, tended to obscure his objectivity. To me these fasts, more than any other of his actions, put in question the very possibility of succeeding in nonviolent action without some kind of coercion. They succeeded against Indians not from the power of truth, but because they could not bear the guilt of causing Gandhi's death, and against the British because they feared the consequences in public disorder if they did not give in.

V

Gandhi's thesis that traditional Indian civilization was less materialistic than that of the modern West is highly debatable. The maharajas whose arrogant display of wealth he had condemned in his speech at Benares were the corrupt survivors of a tradition that allowed power, material wealth, and all varieties of sensual enjoyment to those whose karma had selected them as rulers. There had been isolated monarchs like Asoka who may—the record on him is equivocal —have eschewed the material rewards of power, and in each generation there had been instances of princes accepting austere personal disciplines, though, as in the case of the Emperor Aurangzeb, this might be no improvement, since the abandonment of physical pleasure might mean an increase in the lust for autocratic power. But even such doubtful cases were exceptional. A self-indulgent autocracy was one of the symptoms of decadence that had made India an easy prey to Western imperialists in the eighteenth century.

Yet, if Gandhi's views of the Indian past were highly romanticized in their exaggeration of its antimaterialism, there is no doubt that in some other respects he himself was the final and perhaps the best product of the old India extended into the modern world. The duality he presented to his contemporaries still provides the best clue to the understanding of Gandhi as a political being. In his development to the point of logical extremity of a philosophy of nonviolence he united the insights of ancient Jain holy men and modern Western thinkers, but in his application of that synthetic philosophy he utilized a recognition of political realities that in ancient India, despite the value laid on spirituality, had been frankly accepted as necessary for life in the phenomenal world.

Long ago, before the birth of Christ, a treatise on political method called the *Arthashastra* was compiled by a certain Kautilya, said to have been minister of the Emperor Chandragupta; its doctrines of political expediency were passed down from generation to generation in those Indian realms that remained more or less autonomous, and there can be little doubt that in his childhood, as son of the Prime Minister of Porbandar and later of Rajkot, Gandhi grew up in a setting where this ancient lore was still current in a form diluted by centuries of vassalage to the Moslems and the British. Destiny may not have allowed Mohandas Gandhi to follow his father, Kamarchand, as the political head of a petty state in Kathiawar; it did give him as a late-ripening gift the political astuteness of the Gandhis. And, while one looks vainly in his acts for the appalling cynicism that Kautilya's *Arthashastra* bequeathed to centuries of Indian rulers and their dewans and viziers, the political subtlety is still there.

For, in his superb sense of timing, in his quick intuitive grasp of the balance of forces, in his instinct for effective symbolic action, and in his grasp of the strategy of struggle, Gandhi was one of the most able politicians of his time, and all the more remarkable because, remembering the lessons of the Bhagavad Gita, he never sought for the rewards of politics. To be a ruler did not interest him. To manipulate the intangible elements of power did. So he became the destroyer of an empire, and in the process felt that he was doing nothing contrary to his dharma, his religious duty. For to him every act of life had spiritual implications, and the secular acts that might damn or save us were, by that very token, as religious as the rituals of those who styled themselves holy men.

Thus, when Gandhi finally declared his political war of *Satyagraha* on the British, he was perhaps more faithful to the real traditions of his country than when he called up the symbolism of the spinning wheel with its Edenic myth of a peasant Golden Age. Yet one essential difference remained between Gandhi and Kautilya. If Gandhi accepted politics as an inevitable part of the duty of a religious man, he believed that this could only work if the politics were completely irradiated by the religion. The *Arthashastra* had been as shaped by the doctrine of ends justifying means, as in the writings of Machiavelli; in the eyes of Kautilya the political present was the prisoner of the future goal. For Gandhi the future was the emergent of the living present, the end shaped inevitably by the means, and he had that courage rare among politicians (but an element of political genius where it exists) to abandon an action when the means becomes distorted; that, in his view, was the very essence of an "experiment with Truth."

Gandhi's political realism was strikingly evident in his changing attitude toward the British rule in India. He had no shred of the sentimentality that characterizes emotional nationalism. If it could be proved that British rulers were incapable of giving Indians a life of freedom and dignity, then they must go. But while there remained a chance that their presence might be compatible with justice to Indians, he could not, on his return to India, see any point in replacing them by native rulers of the same kind.

This is the explanation for what were often regarded as Gandhi's glaring inconsistencies of policy during 1918 and 1919. In 1918 he was so willing to cooperate with the British authorities that he attended a meeting called by the Viceroy, Lord Chelmsford, and even agreed to assist the British in building up the Indian army. On this occasion he assured Chelmsford that his own victory in Champaran had been a demonstration of "the ultimate sovereignty of British justice," and he went on to assure the Viceroy that if he could only popularize the idea of *Satyagraha* he could present "an India that would defy the whole world." It was, after that, something of an anticlimax to act as a recruiting sergeant, and he was unsuccessful in this role, which temporarily diminished his popularity in Congress and allowed those who advocated violent tactics to gain more influence than they might otherwise have done.

It was because of anxiety over the growth of terrorism that the British government in India, which had overreacted toward dissent ever since the Indian Mutiny, decided to implement the report of a commission headed by Justice Rowlatt that in July 1918 had recommended heavy penalties and secret trial without appeal for anyone suspected of terrorism or even of having in his possession what might be interpreted as a seditious document. During the interval between the commission's report and the passing of the Rowlatt Bill in March 1919, nationalists of all views were united in their opposition, and when Gandhi, still convalescent from a nervous breakdown complicated by dysentery, rejected the British arguments and began to tour the country preaching a nation-wide *Satyagraha* against the Rowlatt Bill, it seemed natural for them to follow the one Indian leader whose tactics had—in South Africa—produced positive results.

This was Gandhi's real entry into active Indian politics, for his actions in Champaran and Ahmedabad had been essentially social in aims and tactics. Like the gleam of light that told him to fast at Ahmedabad, the inspiration of a dream told him "that we should call upon the country to observe a general hartal." The hartal was a traditional Indian form of nonviolent protest, a kind of general strike in which merchants would close their stores and workers down their tools, and the empty bazaars and workshops would express a silent protest against a ruler who had acted unjustly.

The Satyagraha Sabha was founded in Bombay to plan the action, which would begin immediately the Rowlatt Bill became law. Local committees were set up all over India, and volunteers were recruited to break the laws; they were expected to fast and pray beforehand as a purification.

From the beginning the nonviolent nature of the campaign was stressed. Gandhi served notice on the violent revolutionaries that he did not intend to be their tool when, on the eve of the hartal, he pronounced against Communism, equating it with other aspects of what he regarded as the corruption of the West. "Bolshevism is the necessary result of modern civilization. Its insensate worship of matter has given rise to a school which has been brought up to look upon materialistic advancement as the goal and which has lost all touch with the final things in life."

The measures to be used in the Rowlatt *Satyagraha* largely set the pattern for later nonviolent campaigns against the British. Apart from the hartal and protest processions, *Satyagrahis* were expected to offer themselves for arrest by breaking one of a small group of oppressive laws. They could either contravene the salt-tax law by making salt on the seashore, or sell forbidden books (which included Gandhi's translation of *Unto This Last*), or distribute the unregistered newspaper, *Satyagrahi*, which Gandhi published for the occasion.

The Viceroy was duly warned of the action Gandhi proposed, and this practice was followed in all later campaigns, giving Congress battles with the government the character of tournaments or ritual combats, in which the rules are set, foul blows are forbidden, and the issue rests on the skill, endurance, and sportsmanship of the combatants. The practice, in terms of Gandhian strategy, was not so Quixotic as it may appear. It prevented the movement succumbing to the authoritarianism that is inevitable when conspiratorial methods are used. Since nothing was based on surprise, it allowed Gandhi to move forward and retreat with a great deal more flexibility than is available to the ordinary revolutionary. And, by removing all possible ground for ill feeling on the other side, it left the channels always open for negotiation and compromise.

The response to the call for *Satyagraha* was vast beyond all expectations. It was the first real mass manifestation of the desire of Indians for liberation. Starting in Delhi on March 30 and continuing in the other great cities on April 6, the hartal was almost complete. "Millions" of people are said to have participated in the demonstrations, including Hindus and Moslems, women and schoolchildren. For the first time in Indian history the issue of independence seemed to be moving out of the narrow circle of the educated into the lower classes.

The authorities responded with violence. Police beat demonstrators with steel-tipped staves and in Delhi fired on them. In Punjab, where unrest had been active even before the *Satyagraha*, mob violence broke out, and Gandhi, setting off from Bombay in the hope of calming the situation, was turned back by the British. There were outbreaks of violence in other parts of the country, and then, on April 13, the most shocking event in India since the Mutiny occurred. Brigadier-General Dyer in Amritsar ordered his Gurkhas and Baluchis to fire into the crowd assembled for a demonstration in the Jallianwala Bagh; 379 people were killed and more than a thousand were wounded.

Gandhi was appalled by the violence on both sides that appeared to have been set off by a movement that aimed at victory by nonviolence, by the power of Truth. He fasted for three days in penance, and then, on April 18, called off the *Satyagraha*, admitting he had committed "a Himalayan blunder" by encouraging the untrained masses to take part in a movement that required the highest training in self-control.

Yet the movement, though it had taken a disastrous turn from the point of view of the strict *Satyagrahi*, had not been a total failure. It had brought the issue of independence out of the conclaves of Congress and the cells of terrorists and into the streets and houses of India. It had revealed, through the actions of the fanatical Dyer, the basis of brute force on which the British rule was founded. At the same time it had forced the authorities to reconsider their tactics, so that in practice the Rowlatt Act was never invoked, and other similar bills were not passed into law.

Gandhi himself had learned a notable lesson. In places where there were volunteers with training, there had been no violence. It had only occurred where there were no volunteers or where they had been arrested. It was clear that every *Satyagraha* in future must be clearly delimited and led by reliable and dedicated workers. For the rest, by retiring before the situation had degenerated too far, Gandhi had not only exhibited the steadfastness of his own nonviolent principles; he had also performed a skillful tactical withdrawal that would enable him to plan more effective action.

The three years following the abandonment of the Rowlatt *Satyagraha* mounted into a period of intense activity as Gandhi secured the effective leadership of Congress and moved into new areas of agitation to widen support for the continuing campaign for independence which now, having recognized the true face of imperial power, he knew to be necessary. Some of his actions, such as his involvement in the Khilafat campaign, were little more than clever maneuvers. He can really have cared little whether the Sultan of Turkey remained Caliph (and in any case the whole agitation was to disintegrate when the Turks themselves decided to depose and expel the Commander of the Faithful), but he realized that British efforts to abolish the Caliphate had stirred resentment among Indian Moslems,

and by showing his sympathy for them—as a Hindu—
he won a Moslem following, particularly among the
Pathans, and brought large numbers of them into Congress. By the time Congress met at Nagpur in 1920 to
demand independence "within the British Empire if
possible, or outside it if necessary," it was stronger and
more representative than ever before. It had rejected
the British attempts to persuade the Indian people to
accept Dyarchy (which meant that Indians would control local affairs, but the British would retain the crucial
posts and dictate general policies), and it had accepted
Gandhi's plan to transform it into a disciplined nonviolent organization dedicated to action.

The ambitious target of *swaraj* by the end of 1921
was adopted by the newly militant Congress (in which
Gandhi's ascendancy was confirmed at the death of
Tilak in the summer of 1920), and on August 1, by returning the gold Kaiser-i-Hind medal he had received
for his ambulance work in South Africa, Gandhi
initiated the first stage of a new *Satyagraha*. This was
a campaign of noncooperation with the imperial power.
Other distinguished Indians relinquished their honors,
students stayed away from colleges, prominent lawyers
ceased to practice in British courts and joined Gandhi
as his lieutenants, and in the Northwest Province the
Pathan *Satyagrahis* tried to persuade soldiers to re-
nounce their allegiance.

Meanwhile, Gandhi started the "constructive campaign" aimed at the simplification of Indian life to make
the country worthy of independence. He opened the
first shops for the sale of hand-woven khaddar cloth and
presided over the first of many bonfires in which foreign-
made garments were burned in the streets of Indian
towns. With his usual sense of the dramatic gesture, he

chose this time to abandon even the simple shirt, dhoti, and cap he had been wearing since he gave up European garb, and to adopt a mere loincloth, which fulfilled a triple function: it emphasized simplicity of living, it advertised handmade Indian cloth, and it identified Gandhi himself with the poorest of Indians. In this attenuated costume he traveled for months about India, and these travels were the beginning of his phenomenal popularity among the village people, who saw in this scrawny, half-naked little man, with his great turnip watch and impish smile behind steel-rimmed spectacles, no less than a great sannyasin and perhaps even—as many of them believed—an avatar of Lord Krishna, a deity moving among them. To these people Gandhi's presence meant more than his program, and it is perhaps because their loyalty was based on feeling rather than self-interest that his name still has most resonance when it is spoken by Indian peasants.

It was with the aid of such village people that he planned to move into the next stage of *Satyagraha*. In Bardoli, a district of Gujarat, he proposed to call a mass refusal to pay taxes. The call was delayed by the arrival in Bombay of the Prince of Wales. Congress greeted the Prince with a national hartal and a boycott on all ceremonies, but the movement got out of hand, and in Bombay there was street fighting in which many people were killed. Regarding this as an inauspicious sign, Gandhi postponed the tax strike, even though this meant abandoning the last hope of *swaraj* in 1921. On their side the British were equally disturbed; they suspected that Congress was secretly planning a violent uprising, and in December a series of mass arrests removed to prison the more militant Congress leaders, but not yet Gandhi himself.

In February 1922 Gandhi finally decided to call the tax strike in Bardoli. It would begin, he warned the new Viceroy, Lord Reading, on the eighth of the month; he hoped it would spread from district to district throughout India, with the *Satyagrahis* taking over peacefully as administration disintegrated, until the British became convinced of the untenability of their rule in India. Three days before the eighth, violence erupted again in a particularly horrifying manner. On the occasion of a procession of noncooperators in Gorakhpur, more than twenty policemen were killed by rioters and their bodies thrown into a burning town hall. Once again the masses had demonstrated the limitations of their power to apply *Satyagraha*, and once again, though the Viceroy had shown a willingness to negotiate, Gandhi abandoned a campaign marred by blood. Even at this late hour he was willing to postpone a political success to avoid what he would have regarded as a moral failure.

This was one of the lowest points in Gandhi's career. Once again he had abandoned a *Satyagraha* campaign just when it was reaching its peak, and his followers' morale had been as deeply shaken by this decision as his own by events in Gorakhpur. His influence might have faded completely if the British had not chosen this moment, when he appeared at his weakest, to remove him from the political scene. Nothing could have better suited Gandhi's inner wishes. Both he and India needed a period of separation. "My removal from their midst will be a benefit for the people," he remarked when he was arrested at his ashram on March 10, 1922.

Eight days later he appeared before Magistrate Robert Broomfield of Ahmedabad in an encounter that is still remembered in India as "The Great Trial," not only because it was an important event in the history of liberation, but also because on both sides it was marked by a singular chivalry. Looking back on the event after fifty years, it seems obvious that even at this point Gandhi had begun to win his fight, for it was clear that Broomfield, a veteran of the Indian civil service, shared the uneasiness that afflicted many British officials in India when they were faced by a man of courage and probity who was, in effect, turning against them their own political theories and their own code of honorable behavior. Conversion, the aim of *Satyagraha*, had begun.

Gandhi pleaded guilty. He could have done little else, since the articles in *Young India* on which the charges were based had been deliberately seditious. "We want to overthrow the Government," he had said, and he had described the noncooperation campaign of 1920 as "a fight to the finish." Broomfield, treating his duty as a distasteful exercise in formal legality, emphasized that Gandhi stood in the eyes of many Indians as "a great patriot and a great leader." Sentencing him to six years' imprisonment, he turned the verdict into an accolade by noting that this was the sentence imposed on Gandhi's great predecessor, Tilak. Gandhi remarked on the courtesy he had received, and the trial ended with judge and prisoner bowing solemnly to each other. It was no farce. It was an incident that demonstrated Gandhi's power to arouse the better nature of his opponents, and it showed how closely attuned he was to the influences that, in those vital decades between the wars, were changing the political attitudes of the British people.

vi

"Watch everything. Mend where you can. Be still where you are helpless." So Gandhi wrote in 1925 to his English disciple Madeleine Slade, and the words might serve as epigraph to the years between his imprisonment in the spring of 1922 and his return to intense political activity almost six years later at the end of 1927. It was an interlude, a time of regaining personal strength and reshaping his objectives, during which his attention was devoted less to the political struggle than it was to religion and to the development of a social doctrine, which I shall discuss in the next chapter.

Gandhi entered Yeravda Prison, near Poona, with a great deal of composure. He was already familiar with the predictable routines of prison life, and even if he exaggerated when he told his disciples that he enjoyed jail terms as rest cures, on this occasion he clearly appreciated the detachment in which imprisonment allowed him to consider the alarming tendency for Indian nonviolence movements to create the kind of volatile atmosphere in which violence exploded. His conclusion was that he must concentrate more on the "concrete program" which, in purifying Indian society, would dissipate the social resentments that bred such destructive emotions.

He also wrote in Yeravda an account of the *Satyagraha* movement in South Africa, started his autobiography, spun many hundred yards of cotton yarn, and read more voraciously than at any other time in his life. He read Kipling and Jules Verne, Vaishnavite poems and Tantric treatises, and such many-volumed masterpieces as Gibbon's *Decline and Fall of the Roman Empire*, Motley's *Rise of the Dutch Republic*, and the entire text of the Mahabharata. None of them affected him so deeply as those revelatory works of his youth, *Unto This Last* and *The Kingdom of God Is Within You*. He admired Gibbon, but he thought the Mahabharata superior, because "Truth transcends history," which is a curious but enlightening remark when one remembers that he regarded the Mahabharata as an exemplary myth. Gandhi, like many people brought up in Indian traditions, had little sense of history and little intellectual need for it. It was the present rather than the past or the future that occupied him, and here myths were of far more use than history, as his own life of deliberately symbolic action had demonstrated. The man who could conceive the great war of the Pandavas as an allegory of the battle for good and evil within the human heart was well equipped to carry on a war in which the psychological elements—the renewal of the Indian sense of identity and the erosion of the British sense of righteousness—were far more important than any disposition of physical forces.

Gandhi was indeed to prove eventually his consequent dictum that "nonviolence is made of sterner stuff than armies," but it was clear to him on his unexpected release from prison owing to sickness in February 1924 that the time for realizing it was as yet far from auspicious. Congress had lost strength and unity after the collapse of its irrational hope of achieving *swaraj* in 1921, while the artificial unity between Hindus and Moslems promoted by the Khilafat agitation had collapsed through Kemal Ataturk's abolition of the Caliphate. Communal strife between adherents of the two religions led in September to a massacre of Hindus in Kohat in the Northwest Province, and Gandhi's first important public act after his release was a twenty-one-day fast in protest against the re-emergence of Hindu-Moslem hostility. This resulted in a temporary reconciliation between the leaders of the two religions, but it did nothing to counter the growing strength of the Moslem League, which the British were encouraging as a rival organization to Congress. Even apart from the League, a fragmentation of the movement toward independence was evident, and during the 1920s political forces that are still shaping India began to emerge. The Communists appeared as an independent movement that attracted many of the former terrorist factions; the Hindu Mahasabha, fanatically anti-Moslem, arose to claim the tradition of political orthodoxy founded by Tilak. Gandhi was firmly opposed to both; then, as later, he looked to India as a pluralist country where men of all creeds would live in brotherhood, while he rejected the Communists' theory of the dictatorship of the proletariat as firmly as their willingness to use violence.

Even within Congress there were alarming rifts. One group, led by Motilal Nehru and the Patel brothers, had decided to accept the severely limited opportunities which Dyarchy offered of working for independence within the establishment, and they had founded the Swaraj Party, which won considerable success in the elections. Jawaharlal Nehru and others of the younger leaders opposed them in favor of continuing the non-cooperation policy, and among this group had arisen the demagogic figure of Subhas Chandra Bose (later to become the protégé of the Japanese and of Hitler) whose predilection for talking in terms of bloodshed and strutting in uniform at the head of his corps of militant volunteers Gandhi regarded with intense distrust.

It seemed to Gandhi no time for precipitate action, no time even for standing on the extremities of principle, and in December 1924 he accepted the presidency of Congress merely in order to exercise his talents for compromise and in this way to keep the rival factions from flying apart. He avoided any other political initiative during his year of office, spending most of his time traveling around India to promote khaddar, and founding the All-Indian Spinners' Association. He resigned the presidency with an air of great relief at the end of 1925, and for the rest of his life refused to accept any office in the Congress organization. He also announced that he intended to make 1926 a year of political silence.

The idea of silence as a regenerative force had appealed to Gandhi ever since, thirty years before in South Africa, he had visited a Trappist monastery and had been impressed by the serenity of its discipline. Already he had adopted the custom of keeping every Monday silent in a literal way, communicating where unavoidable by notes scribbled with a pencil stub. His political silence he interpreted as involving a virtual retreat into his ashram at Sabarmati, where he passed his time in meditation, in sharing the necessary toil of the community, in holding prayer meetings, and in talking to the visitors who arrived not only from many parts of India but also from Europe and the United States. If they wished to stay, they had to accept the austere discipline of the ashram; Gandhi had retained from his interlude in Britain a fanatical insistence on punctuality and cleanliness, and his Bania background emerged in a hatred of waste and in the introduction of book-keeping practices that accounted for the last anna received and spent. Many thought it worth the mental and physical discomfort in order to share Gandhi's thoughts and participate in the ecumenical rituals of the ashram.

It was during these years that Gandhi developed his international reputation as a religious teacher; while the English and American wanderers in search of spiritual peace treated him as a guru, the aboriginal Gonds of central India had begun to worship him as a member of their tribal pantheon. Gandhi claimed to relish neither godhead nor guruhood, yet his very choice of the life style of an Indian rishi, or holy sage, wandering in poverty or living in his hermitage among his chosen disciples, led inevitably to such identifications. Indeed, even in political terms, it is difficult to explain, except by using Indian religious terminology, the decisive influence that Gandhi wielded in Congress without holding—except for a single year—

any official position in its hierarchy. His relationship was in fact that of guru not only to Congress as a whole but also specifically to Nehru. It was a role peculiarly Indian and surely unique in the history of revolutions, national or social: in all other revolutionary movements the link between the leader and the party has been institutionalized; in India the leader remained free as a kind of intermediary between the party and the people and also, as Gandhi certainly saw it, between the party and God.

Gandhi's political withdrawal came to an abrupt end in October 1927, when, with other Indian leaders, he received a summons to confer in Delhi with the Viceroy, Lord Irwin. When the Indians appeared, Irwin told them that the British government would send a commission headed by Sir John Simon to visit India and report on the possibility of constitutional changes. The commission had been appointed without consultation with the Indians, and it would contain no Indian representative. It would be responsible solely to Parliament in Westminster, which Irwin and his masters at home regarded as the body responsible for determining the future of India.

The experience brought Gandhi back to politics in a fighting mood. The Simon Commission must be rejected as a denial of the right of Indians to decide their own destiny, and when it arrived on February 3, 1928, it was indeed boycotted by all Indian parties, including the Moslem League and the Hindu Mahasabha. Gandhi considered the time now opportune to call the tax strike at Bardoli that he had planned seven years before, and he authorized Vallabhai Patel to lead it. He used the occasion to make a statement that for the first time extended the scope of his aims beyond India. In South

Africa he had ignored the claims of the black majority
and had defended merely the Indians. "My ambition is
much higher than independence," he now said.
"Through the deliverance of India I seek to deliver the
so-called weaker races from the crushing heels of Western exploitation in which England is the greater
partner." For the first time he was seeing himself in the
role that—among so many others—was actually his: a
pioneer in the destruction of the whole imperial system.

The tax strike at Bardoli was an almost flawless
example of *Satyagraha* in action, and, more important,
the first completely successful civil-disobedience campaign against the actual government of India. Despite
arrests and distraints carried out in a very brutal
manner, the eighty-four thousand peasants of the area
avoided violence and remained firm in their refusal to
pay taxes. In less than six months, after a national
hartal in support of the people of Bardoli, the government gave in, released all prisoners, and appointed a
commission of inquiry that granted the reduction in
taxes that the peasants had demanded and made com-
pensation for the seizure of goods.

Encouraged by such a success for Gandhian tactics,
Congress in December 1928 passed a resolution demanding independence within a year. By December 1929 it
was evident that Ramsay Macdonald's hints of the
possibility of dominion status were unlikely to material-
ize because of political factors in Britain, and Congress,
meeting in Lahore, resolved on complete severance from
the empire. All members were called to resign from
legislatures and official positions. Nehru was elected
president of Congress, and Gandhi was deputed to lead
the nationwide *Satyagraha* that would implement the
resolution. He was to decide its scope and its timing.

On January 26, now celebrated as a national festival, Gandhi published the Indian Declaration of Independence, a document that wedded the purely political ambitions of many of his associates in Congress with his own conception of a liberation that would be social and spiritual as well. As one realizes on reading its bitter rhetoric, he had traveled far in mind since the time, a mere twelve years ago, when he still believed that the British Empire worked for the good of the peoples over whom it ruled. "The British government of India," he said after the predictable preamble about inalienable human rights, "has not only deprived the Indian people of their freedom but has based itself on the exploitation of the masses, and has ruined India economically, politically, culturally and spiritually. We believe, therefore, that India must sever the British connection and attain Purna Swaraj or Complete Independence."

Gandhi was in no hurry to initiate the *Satyagraha*; when he did, the form he chose was a surprise even to his own associates in Congress, many of whom derided his plan. Yet to take a limited objective had always been one of the basic rules of *Satyagraha* as Gandhi conceived it, and the salt tax was for many reasons an excellent target. It was a tax that bore down on the poor, and the issue had historical resonances, for a salt tax had been one of the main grievances that provoked the French Revolution. Not only would resistance to it be popular among the peasants; it was also the kind of feature of British government in India whose exposure would reveal to the English people the impositions that were being carried out regularly in their name. Gandhi was particularly insistent on this point; he emphasized it in the letter that he sent by hand to Lord Irwin, using as messenger the well-known English pacifist Reginald

Reynolds. Addressing the Viceroy as "Dear Friend," he declared his intention not to harm a single Englishman or any legitimate English interest, and then went on to say, "My ambition is no less than to convert the British people through nonviolence, and thus make them see the wrong they have done to India. I do not seek to harm your people. I want to serve them even as I want to serve my own." For all its noble sentiments, the letter was a mildly worded threat, and Irwin predictably contented himself with replying that he regretted Gandhi's decision to embark on action that would bring him into conflict with the law.

Gandhi's course was now quite clear. He intended to rely on cumulative effect, on a movement that would be small in the beginning and almost childishly simple in its aim, but would spread like ripples in a lake until the whole of India was stirred. He set out at dawn on March 12 from Sabarmati Ashram, at the head of seventy-nine volunteers. They were marching to Dandi on the seacoast, two hundred forty-one miles away. Vast crowds accompanied them out of Ahmedabad, and throughout the march the volunteers were only the minute tip of a procession that always numbered several thousands. The Viceroy had ordered a policy of noninterference, since he believed the march would fail. It became instead a triumph, with the villagers strewing the roads with green branches for Gandhi to walk on, and gathering every night in hundreds under the peepul trees to hear him in his thin, small voice expounding the glories of freedom and the beauties of the moral life. The whole enterprise took on in the imagination of observers and participants the quality of a mythical quest, and people from all parts of India and in the rest of the world followed with a tense anticipation—as they followed Lindbergh's flights—the slow, deliberate progress of the little man with his bamboo staff leading his peaceful army to the sea. Gandhi himself lived through those days in the spirit of a legend, immersing himself as deeply as an actor might have done in his role of non-violent general, leading the forces of good to victory over evil like Hanuman in the stories from the Ramayana that he had heard with delight in his childhood. "We are marching in the name of God," he would cry as he entered the villages, and if others saw him as an avatar, he certainly saw himself at this time in almost manic terms as a prophet especially inspired.

The march reached Dandi, and on April 6, the anniversary of the massacre of Jallianwala Bagh, after bathing ceremonially in the ocean, Gandhi came to the shore and picked up a fragment of salt, while the poetess Sarojini Naidu shouted, "Hail, Deliverer!" The effect of that simple gesture was extraordinary. Through the years of stagnation since 1922, the conviction that alien rule must be brought to an end had been spreading among Indians of all classes, while the steady work of Gandhi's followers had resulted in a wider understanding of the necessary disciplines of *Satyagraha*. When Gandhi picked up his pinch of salt, it was like turning a switch that sets in motion some vast and complex mechanism. Everywhere in India people began to manufacture salt, on beaches, on houseroofs, and to hawk it in the streets. Legislators and local officials resigned; hundreds of village headmen left their posts. Newspapers ceased publication rather than accept censorship. There were the usual hartals and processions, policed by nonviolent volunteers. Up in Peshawar the men of the Garhwali Rifles, one of the crack regiments of the Indian Army, refused to fire on the demonstrators, and for two weeks, until Gurkha troops arrived, the city was a free commune administered nonviolently by the local Gandhian leader, Khan Abdul Ghaffar Khan, and his Red Shirts. Women joined the movement in unprecedented numbers, even emerging from purdah to do so. This time there was no violence to mar the *Satyagraha*; as Gandhi had promised, not a single Englishman was hurt.

If Gandhi and his followers believed that this would be the end of British power, they were mistaken. The government arrested sixty thousand people, and harshly suppressed the movement in Peshawar. Most of the Congress leaders were in prison, but Gandhi still had thousands of trained volunteers to direct, and he now warned that the *Satyagraha* would assume a more active character than ever before by the nonviolent invasion of government salt factories. The threat brought his arrest on May 4, but this did not halt the movement, for Gandhi had arranged for that eventuality. His detention without trial under an old East India Company statute provoked a countrywide hartal, and on May 21 his followers invaded the Dharasana Saltworks. It was an impressive example of nonviolent tactics. The twenty-five hundred chosen volunteers advanced like a miniature army, with their commissariat and their ambulance corps of stretcher-bearers and first-aid men. Four hundred armed police guarded the saltworks. Like Indian policemen even today, they became easily un-nerved under stress, and as the *Satyagrahis* advanced in wave after wave, they attacked them with a blind mechanical violence. Many of the demonstrators suffered from fractured skulls, some died, and hundreds were hospital cases. The struggle ended with the salt-works still unoccupied, but even though they failed, it was the courage of the *Satyagrahis*, described by American and British journalists that impressed the world.

This was the climax of the movement. One hundred thousand people were in prison, the elite of Congress, and resistance moved into low key, as continued noncooperation, so that Bombay and other towns were virtually in the hands of Gandhian shadow governments. The Viceroy, like Gandhi, believed that a stalemate had been reached that could only be resolved by establishing a dialogue, and on January 26, 1931, he released the Congress leaders and invited Gandhi to confer with him in Delhi. Out of days of conversation emerged the face-saving Irwin-Gandhi Pact. Salt, it was agreed, could be made for personal use; the hundred thousand imprisoned volunteers would be released; Gandhi would represent Congress at the Round Table Conference to be held in London to determine the next stage in giving constitutional government to India.

The immediate gains were slight, for when Gandhi reached London he found that the Round Table Conference mirrored the rich confusion of Indian society. There were representatives of Moslems and Sikhs and Christians, of untouchables and Eurasians, of princes and parties and planters, and though Gandhi contended (with excusable exaggeration) that he represented eighty-five per cent of Indians, his voice was lost in the clamor of conflicting interests. The Conference seemed obsessed with the problems of safeguarding minorities to the exclusion of what appeared to Gandhi the basic issue of independence. He suspected the British of exaggerating divisions that in a free India would easily resolve themselves; as events in the subcontinent since 1947 have demonstrated, he greatly underestimated the divisive factors of creed and language in a country he chose to regard as a unity. Here, ironically, the Western influences on Gandhi's thinking emerged, for a united India (though vaguely adumbrated in ancient times) was in practical and historical terms a British concept.

Gandhi's real achievement on his visit to England in 1931 was the extraordinary sympathy that he aroused among the working people in the East End of London and in the Lancashire textile towns, where his Swadeshi campaign was throwing weavers out of work. He seemed to them an Oriental version of Charlie Chaplin's little man, and from that time "Old Gandhi" was remembered as a personality and his cause supported by the common people who one day in the future would send to Westminster a government committed to dismantling the empire.

He returned at the end of 1931, after visits to Romain Rolland and Mussolini, to find in power a new and harsher Viceroy, Lord Willingdon. The policy of repression had returned. Nehru and other Congress leaders were in prison. On January 4, 1932, Gandhi was himself arrested and again detained without trial. His attention shifted away from the issue of independence to that of untouchability, and he entered another of his periods of reclusion from Congress. Not until 1940 did he again exert himself as an active political force.

Yet though the immediate results appeared so meager, the Salt Satyagraha deserves amply the place it now holds in the mythology of India's liberation. It immensely raised the self-respect of Indians and their confidence that they could not only liberate their country but could also govern it when it was free. Never had so many people shown themselves so willing to suffer for the cause; never had such exemplary discipline been shown; never had so large a campaign been carried on without breaking down into violence; never had women and peasants been so deeply involved; never before had there been examples, as in Peshawar and, to a less extent, in Bombay, of a virtual assumption of local government by *Satyagrahis*.

As for the British, in England itself Gandhi's presence had given them for the first time a sense of personal involvement in the fate of India. And among the sahibs, such events as the disobedience of the Garhwali Regiment aroused the old anxieties of the days of the great Mutiny; it seemed once again as if they could no longer rely on native soldiers or policemen to protect their rule. The feeling that India was rejecting them could produce the kind of sensitive reaction evident in Judge Broomfield's attitude at Gandhi's trial in 1921, but it would also produce the fear-bred brutality of the British police officers who directed the defense of Dharasana in 1930. Both were symptoms of insecurity. Though Gandhi failed at the Round Table Conference and returned to find resistance temporarily eclipsed by repression, the Salt March and its consequences had propelled the British Raj a stage nearer its end.

vii

Rejecting the epithet of a saint acting as a politician, Gandhi once defined himself as a politician trying to be a saint. If a concern for the collective life of man on this earth is what constitutes a politician, regardless of his religious preoccupations, then in every sense Gandhi qualified for the title. He was a politician when he strove for the civil rights of Indians in South Africa; he was a politician when he dedicated himself to the ending of British rule in India; he was a politician when he envisaged a total transformation of the structure of Indian society and the displacement of the British Raj, not by an Indian imitation of it operated by those whom Mulk Raj Anand has called the Brown Sahibs but by Ram Raj, the kingdom of God on earth, the millennial realm of peace and justice.

Gandhi has often been accused, particularly

by Marxists, of reformism and gradualism. The two terms are not identical in meaning, and it would probably be just to dismiss the label of reformist, since Gandhi did demand radical changes within men as well as in their relations, and to define him rather as a gradualist revolutionary, since what he wanted to create in the end was a society different not only from that imposed by the British but also from what remained, by the end of the nineteenth century, of traditional Hindu society.

It was the method—not the result—that was deliberately gradualist. In the prayer meetings for sympathizers of all religions that he instituted early in his South African campaign, Gandhi insisted that Christian devotional hymns be sung with those of the Vaishnavas, and for many years, until it was replaced by "When I survey the wondrous cross," his favorite was John Henry Newman's "Lead, kindly light," which it seemed to him contained within a single sentence the substance of the whole program he had evolved. "I do not ask to see/ The distant scene: one step enough for me."

The "one-step-enough-for-me" approach was in complete accordance with the general philosophy of *Satyagraha* and also with the teachings of the Bhagavad Gita as Gandhi interpreted them. "Renunciation of the fruits of action," he once explained in introducing the Gita to one of his Western friends, "does not mean that there can be no fruits. But no action must be undertaken for the sake of its fruits." This was in accordance with the basic philosophy of *Satyagraha*, which was a seeking of truth; the *Satyagrahi*, aiming to convert his opponent, must always himself remain open to conversion. *Satyagraha* accepts certain essential principles as beyond dispute, but its exponents developed these principles experimentally in the world of action, where everything is relative and mutable, and in this sense the Gandhian philosophy is one of endless becoming, which makes it —in a somewhat different way from left-wing Marxism —a doctrine of permanent revolution. No society can ever be perfect, because perfection is an attribute of the Absolute alone, and for this reason the *Satyagrahi* cannot accept the rigid plans of the utopian theorist, since he has to be sensitive to the constantly changing demands of human relations, and these assail him, not in the future, but now and here.

This attitude parallels that of the anarchists, who have always held that our present responsibility is to get rid of social and political institutions that are obviously bringing neither freedom nor social justice to mankind in general, but who have also claimed that it is not for men in the present to plan in rigid detail the world in which future men—who will be different because they will be freed from the restrictions that shape even revolutionaries in our world—will wish to live. Yet, by the very process of condemning certain aspects of existing society, the anarchists implicitly indicated the kind of world they might accept, and some of them and of those who stood near to them—writers like Kropotkin and Tolstoi, William Morris and Aldous Huxley—went so far as to proffer tentative sketches of the kind of society in which they thought men could live in peace and open to a benign light the fullness of their natures. Since Gandhi defined himself more than once as a kind of anarchist, it is not surprising to find that the society he outlines fragmentarily in his articles and speeches is remarkably similar even in detail to that of other libertarian writers, and just as distant as theirs from the centralized and industrialized utopias of the Marxists and other authoritarian socialists.

Gandhi's social vision is really arranged in a number of planes that recede from action in the present to a program for the immediate future and thence to a tentative sketch of "the distant scene," based carefully and closely on existing social realities.

Into the closest plane fit his most urgent preoccupations during the last two decades of his life. In the 1930s his main concern was for the untouchables, whom he called the Harijans, or Children of God. Gandhi did not entirely abandon the caste system, since he believed that originally it was not a system of privilege but a way of arranging duties. The hierarchical aspect of caste, which placed the Brahmin at the head and the untouchables beneath contempt, was in his view a late excrescence; to stir the consciences of Hindus he staged during the 1930s two great fasts, and in 1933 went on a pilgrimage of twelve thousand miles, in the hope that he could close by persuasion the atrocious rift between the twice-born and those whose very presence was supposed to pollute them. He transformed his own ashram at Sabarmati into a center for training untouchables and edited a paper called *Harijan*, to which he contributed most of his later writings.

If the removal of the worst features of the caste system occupied Gandhi during the 1930s, in the next decade events forced him to give most of his attention to another of his cherished doctrines, the brotherhood of all religious men. He believed that religion was a private matter, that each man made his own approach to God, and that the attempt to create a religious state was as unacceptable as any other way of differentiating between men who had found various ways of describing their spiritual aspirations and experiences. The inter-communal massacres at the time of India's liberation made this the most urgent problem of Gandhi's last years, and his attempt to solve it by an unhappy pilgrim-age through the regions troubled by religious strife was eventually to bring him to his death at the hands of a religious fanatic.

To the vision of a society without social or religious discrimination that these preoccupations suggest, one must add another distinctive concern of Gandhi's last two decades, his practical efforts to rehabilitate the Indian village. In 1934 he created the All-Indian Village Industries Association to widen the economic basis of rural life, and in 1936 he settled down in the remote village of Segaon, not far from Vinoba Bhave's ashram of Wardha in the Deccan. He changed its name event-ually to Sevagram, the Village of Service, and there he began a series of practical experiments in ways of reviving agriculture, industry, education, and other features of the rural culture of India.

In concerning himself so closely with untouchability, communal reconciliation, and village rehabilitation, Gandhi was in fact giving expression on a limited scale to the "constructive program" that he had always re-garded as the essential complement to the nonviolent struggle for liberation from British rule. The aim of the program—the second plane of Gandhi's social vision—was to achieve the collective purification without which liberation from the British would not make India free. Hindus and Moslems as well as the British had shared in the devastation of the village culture of traditional India, and together they must dedicate themselves to the measures necessary for its reconstruction.

The constructive program in its most elaborated form consisted of eighteen items that together would bring about a thorough reformation of Indian society at its basic level, in the rural areas. Communal reconciliation and the removal of untouchability headed the list, and prohibition, following immediately afterward, indicated the puritanical character of the Gandhian society; it might not expect religious uniformity, but it would impose rules of moral behavior.

The hand-making of cloth from locally grown materials and the development of other village industries came next in the order of importance, since Gandhi realized that no rural culture could survive without a sound decentralized economic basis. Education, in his view, must be associated with the development of handcrafts, for children should learn first how to use their hands, and only then should they receive literary education. This "basic education" must as far as possible be self-supporting through the sale of the products of work done during vocational training; in this way children could learn one of the essential rules of the Gandhian life—that every man must perform "bread-labor" in field or workshop to meet his material needs. Education should not end with childhood; Gandhi advocated programs of adult training, not merely to enable illiterates to catch up but as a permanent feature, so that men's minds would be enriched continually, from infancy until death. One aspect of both kinds of education would be the fostering of a love of one's vernacular and of the national common language, which Gandhi believed should be Hindi. (He did not foresee the furies that would erupt in southern India during the 1960s because of the attempt to impose this northern language on Tamils and Malayalis.)

Indian villages, at least within historical memory, have been unhealthy places, ill-drained, muddy in the monsoons, dusty in the dry season, and infested with mosquitos that breed in the stagnant ponds and with flies that carry many diseases owing to the lack of the most elementary ideas of sanitation. Gandhi attached importance to the introduction of well-paved lanes and good drainage, and especially of well-kept latrines. He advocated education in hygiene and the introduction of nature-cure clinics that—with cleanliness and proper diet—would obviate the need for modern medicine.

"Service of backward tribes" and "uplift of women" stood fairly high among the items of the constructive program. Though Gandhi called for a simplification of life that his critics have dismissed as mere atavism, he was not a primitivist, and, as his very use of the word "backward" suggests, he did not regard India's aborigines as noble savages. He believed that man had reached the golden age in a village world where he combined good farming with a level of craftsmanship that afforded a sufficient but not a luxurious life; he would have appreciated Hesiod if he had read him. Like the peasants themselves he distrusted the nomad hunter as much as the city sophisticate, and his real desire was to turn the tribes of India into self-supporting farmers.

Women he regarded as, next to untouchables, the most exploited class of India. He held that men and women were complementary—equal in status, but different in function, and he demanded the abolition of purdah, child marriage, and all the other customs that discriminated against women. Women were among his most devoted disciples, and toward the end of his life he placed progressively greater confidence in them and made them his closest companions. He believed very strongly that once women were liberated from male exploitation they would develop a high degree of sexual restraint, and that thus they would solve India's population problem without the introduction of birth control, which he abhorred as an encouragement to indulgences that would destroy the self-control essential to a non-violent society.

In some villages, even in Gandhi's life, a great deal of the constructive program was put into practice, and since then his disciples have developed hundreds of model villages in which local industries based on locally produced raw materials, good sanitation, basic education and the diminution of purdah and untouchability, together with training in better farming methods, have produced a superior standard of living and a sense of increased dignity among the people. When I traveled in 1961 in the Jat villages of what is now Haryana, the difference between those where Gandhian volunteers had been working and those in their unregenerate filth and poverty was remarkable. But even then, thirteen years after Gandhi's death, as the volunteers admitted to me, only fifteen hundred out of India's seven hundred thousand villages had been rehabilitated by them. It is true that the constructive program influenced other Indian projects for village rehabilitation, including many government-sponsored community-development projects, but even counting these, only a small minority of India's rural masses has been touched in any important way by the constructive program Gandhi launched half a century ago. Many millions of Indian villagers actually live today on a lower level of existence than their fathers did under the British. In liberated India Gandhi's social gospel has never been taken seriously by more than a few idealists; the abandonment of the constructive pro-

gram has paralleled the abandonment of nonviolence
by a native ruling class divided between a cynical dedication to self-interest and a soulless doctrinaire socialism.

One feature of the constructive program that Gandhi
implied rather than stated was the presence of the *Satyagrahis*, trained volunteers who serve as teachers, healers,
agricultural advisers, peacemakers, latrine superintend-
ents, and general servants of the people. Bound to
chastity, temperance, and vegetarianism, forbidden to
own possessions, obliged to earn their food by "bread-
labor," they formed a nonviolent elite in the Gandhian
scheme rather like the guardians of Plato's Republic.
When one meets them in the flesh, their virtues give
them a certain disconcerting arrogance: Gandhi's pride
of the spirit, but usually without his charm and humor,
without the dancing originality of mind with which he
filled the bare places he loved. Some of Gandhi's close
followers have been great men in their own right;
Vinoba Bhave and Jayaprakash Narayan were among
them. Most of the volunteers were what Gandhi made
them, and the mold, one senses, was too austere for
ordinary men.

From the plane of the constructive program with its
scheme of villages reformed by a dedicated order of
Satyagrahis, there is a logical progress to the final plane
of Gandhi's social vision, for there the village becomes
the essential unit in a society where urban life seems
to be eliminated by ignoring it. Gandhi hated the great
cities that had grown up in India under the British, and
he must have assumed that in his village world they
would wither away, for he never brings them into his
calculations as features of the world he would like to
see tomorrow.

It is in his discussion of the ideal village-based society

that Gandhi's anarchistic leanings are most strongly expressed. "The State," he says, "represents violence in a concentrated and organized form"; the thought echoes in different ways throughout his writings. When he advocates self-government, he delimits his position carefully by insisting that "self-government means continuous effort to be free of government control, whether it is foreign or whether it is national." "The ideally non-violent state," he also says, "will be an ordered anarchy."

To him the kind of state that can be accepted is no more than a coordinating mechanism in a decentralized society where each village will be a little republic, economically self-sufficient and politically autonomous. A man's duty will be to his immediate neighbors—to the village, in fact—and in service to them he will find his fulfillment. This localism, Gandhi claims, will paradoxically be the guarantee of universalism, and he expresses the thought in an image that conveys with great eloquence the combined looseness and intimacy of the society he foresees.

> In this structure composed of innumerable villages . . . life will not be a pyramid with the apex sustained by the bottom. But it will be an oceanic circle whose centre will be the individual always ready to perish for the village, the latter ready to perish for the circle of villages, till at last the whole becomes one life composed of individuals. . . . The outermost circumference will not wield power to crush the inner circle but will give strength to all within and derive its own strength from it.

Economically the village-based society will tend toward equality, for "violence is bred in inequality." Craftsmen will be their own masters and only those who work the land will be left in possession of it. "No man should have more land than he needs for his dignified sustenance." Farming and handcrafts will be the basis of the economy, but Gandhi does not entirely reject mechanization. He is ready to allow electricity in the villages to give power for tools and simple machines (preferably made locally), but each village should have its own power station to protect its autonomy. Centralized industry should be restricted to a small minimum. The few factories that remain can be left in the hands of their owners as trustees, with the workers sharing equally in control.

Gandhi distrusted the parliamentary system. Even in Britain it seemed to him distant from the people, and to imagine several hundred million Indians electing a few hundred representatives was to him absurd. In its place he substituted a plan for indirect democracy. Each village would be ruled by its own panchayat (the traditional five-man council) and would elect a representative to the district council. Each district council would elect a representative to the regional council, and so on up to the highest council in the nation. There would be few duties for that highest council in an almost completely decentralized society. Even its national functions would largely have devolved into the control of voluntary associations, and it would have little more to do than control communications, power resources, minerals, and forests on behalf of the people.

The army would come to an end. "Militarization of India would mean self-destruction," Gandhi warned in 1947. If the land were invaded, the peace brigades would go out to meet the opponent and resist him nonviolently. Police would exist, and on occasion might even have to use restraint, but punishment would end, and prisons would be places of education. Arbitration, preferably by neighbors, would replace litigation in civil disputes.

Gandhi remains anarchistic rather than anarchist; he never makes the final step into the completely cooperative society. Attenuated as it is, the state still exists; sometimes he even seems to envisage a coercive function for it to perform, when he talks of the expropriation of industries whose owners fail to carry on their duty as trustees. Yet even here he inserts a qualification that places him outside the current of orthodox socialism and nearer to the anarchists. "I look upon an increase in the power of the state with the greatest fear because, while apparently doing good by minimizing exploitation, it does the greatest harm to mankind by destroying individuality, which lies at the root of all progress."

The disquieting feature of Gandhi's ideal society is that, while it rejects political coercion, it appears to rely on strong moral pressures. Duty is stressed constantly; only the performance of duty confers rights, we are told. And while Gandhi salutes the idea of individual judgment being of prime importance and remarks that "in matters of conscience the law of the majority has no place," there is incessant talk in his writings of restraint of various kinds, whether in terms of "willing submission to social restraint for the sake of the well-being of the whole society," or arbitrary restraint through prohibition, or self-restraint through sexual continence or avoidance of the pleasures of the palate.

Gandhi was conscious from his own experience of the creative power of inhibitions; his life was a glorious series of successful sublimations. What he would not allow himself to realize was that, just as prisons create criminals, so restraint and repression can often breed monstrous passions. A society bound by such moral manacles as Gandhi would have men impose on themselves might develop tensions more intense and dangerous than those of societies where restraint is externalized. To such possibilities Gandhi—who was a great self-explorer and should have known better from the storms in his own being—seems to have blinded himself almost deliberately. He never, for example, appears to have thought at all deeply about the roots in German social restraints out of which sprang the Nazi atrocities, or to have related the outbursts of unexampled cruelty in his own country between 1946 and 1948 to the age-old social pressures that found sudden and appalling release as the power of the Raj faded away.

viii

As Gandhi once remarked, in this life the ideal is never achieved. And those who seek to realize the ideal die either in the loneliness of unfulfillment or in the solitude of having betrayed the ideal for an illusion of fulfillment. The latter fate was Lenin's and Nehru's; it awaits Mao Tsetung and Castro. The other fate, of dying alone, unfulfilled but essentially uncorrupted, was that of Kropotkin and Che Guevara and Zapata; it was also, despite all his triumphs, that of Gandhi. His successes were immense if one judges them by the goals of the majority of men; judged by his own aspirations, he failed, yet his failure was a sign of the magnitude of his vision.

The last years of his life—and I would date them from his return to India in 1932—were marked by the two complementary themes of power and sacrifice.

"Nonviolence," Gandhi once said, "does not seize power. It does not even seek power. Power accrues to it." One must not, in other words, desire power; one may accept it. This brings us again to the tortuous point of the coercion implicit in nonviolent action, and the force that a single man can apply when he makes his own life-or-death the lever of other men's consciences. Up to the great Salt March, and in the March itself, Gandhi's victories had been won mainly by organizing other people in great campaigns of civil disobedience. From 1932 onward he preferred the course he had followed in Champaran, that of the single *Satyagrahi* generating a moral power that can move the whole world. His most spectacular successes in the last sixteen years of his life were those in which governments, political parties, factions, and their leaders were taught that, in Robert Payne's words, "A fast is a weapon of terror, a bomb with a time fuse."

Managed with a spectacular sense of the drama of sacrifice, Gandhi's fasts generated the force that, on specific and limited issues, can bring other powers to heel. In 1932, when he fasted to ensure that privileges granted to untouchables in the new political structure being worked out for India would not result in perpetuating their separation from the Hindu world, he not only brought all the Indian leaders running to his prison bedside to arrange the compromise that would please him; he even brought the Prime Minister of Britain hurrying from vacation to a Cabinet meeting in far-off Westminster that would approve the crucial concessions. When he fasted against communal fighting in Calcutta in 1947 he not only forced the leaders of the Moslem and Hindu communities into reconciliation for fear they should be responsible for the death of such a holy man; by the strange charisma of his weakening presence he also attracted to him the leaders of the assassin gangs, who knelt before him and vowed to end their killings. And in his last fast in Delhi, from which he returned to life only with difficulty a few days before his final death, he not only reconciled the warring communities within the capital; he also forced an unwilling Indian cabinet to meet in his presence and give up to Pakistan a large sum of money that it had thought of appropriating as a reprisal for the Pakistani invasion of Kashmir.

These were astonishing moral achievements. But one of the consequences of exercising power, however won, is that it isolates those who wield it from those who lack it, and it is significant that in the last decade of his life, though people crowded round him, Gandhi felt an increasing loneliness in the role of the super-*Satyagrahi* that he had assumed. "Let no one say he is a follower of Gandhi," he declared in 1940. "It is enough that I should be my own follower."

Another consequence of acquiring power, even when wielded nonviolently, is that it brings one into potential conflict with all those who are one's rivals in gaining and keeping it. Gandhi's campaigns against untouchability and for the equality of men of all religions in a liberated India inevitably incurred the hatred of orthodox Hindus, who had suffered a temporary political setback with the death of Tilak in 1920 but had begun to revive with the establishment of the Hindu Mahasabha, and who by 1933 felt strong enough to challenge Gandhi where his influence was strongest, in the villages of India. In 1933, when he went on his great pilgrimage to end untouchability, he achieved wide temporary gains and even brought a permanent end to some of the grosser forms of discrimination. Yet, for the first time in his career, he found his own weapons turned against him as squads of orthodox Hindus nonviolently blocked the entrances to temples and picketed his meetings with their black flags of condemnation. Nor was the Hindu resistance expressed only passively; in 1934 no less than three attempts were made on his life by orthodox fanatics, and his fast in protest against this kind of opposition achieved little result, for he completely failed to dissolve the hatred of the militant traditionalists; it merely increased to the point where his destruction became inevitable.

There were other less subterranean movements grasping for power during the 1930s as India moved slowly toward responsible government. In April 1934, anticipating greater concessions from Britain than the Round Table Conference had appeared to offer, Gandhi had called off the civil-disobedience campaign and at the October 1934 meeting of Congress had formally abandoned all pretensions to leadership. In August the following year the Government of India Act was passed by the British parliament, bringing an end to Dyarchy and providing for self-government on a provincial level; the franchise was greatly widened, and thirty million Indians became eligible for the vote. Asked his advice by Congress leaders who longed to enjoy the first fruits of power, Gandhi dryly remarked, "India is still a prison, but the superintendent allows the prisoners to elect the officials who run the jail." In six provinces out of eleven, Congress won clear majorities; in three others it was the leading party. Eventually it formed nine of the provincial governments.

For a brief, intoxicating interlude until war came in 1939, Indians felt that at last they were beginning to control their own destinies, and Congress governments heady with authority called out police forces led by British officers to beat up with lathis other Indians who rioted against them. The chance of acquiring full power led to the polarization of Hindu and Moslem interests, with Jinnah at the head of the Moslem League manipulating his way into a strategic position in Indian politics by the early years of the war. Within Congress itself there appeared radicalisms of the right and left, represented by Bose's Forward Bloc and the Congress Socialist Party; neither of these trends, nor Nehru's more centrist socialism, was favorable to Gandhi's idea of a decentralized peasant society; indeed, the Congress leaders, whether they inclined toward socialism or capitalist democracy, looked to an India that would be largely industrial and generally modernized in a Western manner; in this they followed the same trends as nationalist movements that were emerging in other colonial or semicolonial countries. They were politically shaped by the power that had dominated them, and they had not liberated themselves as far as Gandhi had done from British stereotypes. They were willing to use his constructive program as propaganda for winning peasant votes, but few of them shared his vision of an idyllic rural anarchy looking back to the days before the Moguls.

The very fact that after the 1937 elections Congress possessed a basis of political power made it less amenable to Gandhi's moral power, and during the 1940s one observes a striking fluctuation in his influence, corresponding to the fortunes of Congress. At the beginning, the Viceroy took India into the war without consulting the provincial ministries, which were the obvious representatives of the Indian people. There was no alternative but for the Congress ministers to resign, and the country reverted to the rule of the British governors. At this point Congress still hoped to strike a bargain, and the rest of the leaders brushed aside Gandhi's objections both to the idea that India should raise armed forces and to the idea that Congress should make conditions for any support it chose to give the British. Congress offered cooperation in the war effort, on condition that the British acknowledge India's complete independence and agree to establish a provisional government in Delhi.

When the Viceroy rejected the offer, the Congress leaders, with no prospect of a return to power, turned to Gandhi, and in October 1940 he devised a scheme of individual civil disobedience by which a series of leaders, beginning with Bhave, followed by Nehru, would defy in action the regulations that forbade them to express freely their views on the war. In all, twenty-three thousand *Satyagrahis* were imprisoned, and Gandhi's journal *Harijan* was among the many suspended newspapers. At the end of 1941, as the Japanese swept nearer, the prisoners were released and shortly afterward Stafford Cripps arrived on behalf of the British government to present proposals Gandhi considered unacceptable. In the summer of that year Congress passed its resolution calling on the British to "Quit India" and appointed Gandhi to direct a mass civil-disobedience movement. Immediately he was arrested, with other Congress leaders, and interned in the Aga Khan's palace at Poona. As a result, instead of the nonviolent campaign that he had planned, India suffered several months of sporadic but violent revolt. He was released in 1944 for ill health. It was his last imprisonment. Altogether he had spent more than six years in Indian and South African jails.

He played his part, sometimes directly and sometimes

indirectly, in the negotiations which, after the advent of a postwar Labor government in Britain, led to the final liberation of India. Largely through his influence, the British had grown weary of their empire. But his opinions counted for comparatively little in the final shaping of India's future. Since he believed in the brotherhood of all Indians and in the possibility of a completely secular state with equality for all religious groups, he was completely opposed to partition of the subcontinent, but his powers of conversion failed with Jinnah, the leader of the Moslem League, who refused to accept anything less than a separate state of Pakistan. When Congress agreed to partition, Gandhi felt a deep sense of betrayal and remarked that "thirty-two years of work have come to an inglorious end"; he was thinking of the years since his return in 1915 that he had devoted to the regeneration of an India that—as he had known it—was now being destroyed.

There were other developments that troubled Gandhi in the months that led to independence. He realized that Congress, as it moved toward power, was shedding the nonviolence that had once seemed expedient to its leaders, and that the India it planned had little in common with the peaceful village society he had envisioned. He was aware of the onset of that sickness of political corruption of which Congress has never been able to cure itself; he called on the leaders to avoid the "ungainly skirmish for power" and to turn the organization into "a body of servants of the nation engaged in constructive work, mostly in villages, to achieve social, moral and economic freedom." His voice went unheard.

Since he realized that his moral power was declining as political power became a reality in India, he turned more and more toward the idea of sacrifice that in his mind had always accompanied the thought of moral power. For many years he had been increasingly fascinated by the fate of Christ. In Rome, in 1931, he had gone to the Sistine Chapel and had wept before the crucifix there. Later, on the bare walls of his room at Sevagram the only decoration was a picture of Christ. And at his prayer meetings "Lead, kindly light" was replaced as the favorite Christian hymn by "When I survey the wondrous Cross," in which Isaac Watts portrayed the fusion of Christ's sorrow and love into a sacrifice that calls on men to offer themselves completely.

The ideal of perishing for a cause, for other men, for a village even, occurs more frequently in his writings as time goes on. He had always held that *Satyagraha* implied the willingness to accept not only suffering but also death for the sake of a principle. "Just as one must learn the art of killing in the training for violence, so one must learn the art of dying in the training for nonviolence." He had shown his willingness to die, and had used it as a powerful weapon in his fasts, which succeeded because he was so sincerely and obviously intent on death if he failed to convert his opponent. Increasingly, as his life shortened, he became convinced that some day, sooner rather than later, his death would be demanded of him by the old enemy, violence.

This feeling grew more intense than ever as he saw the evil ghosts of an India he had long thought dead beginning to walk again. Out of the past of the thugs and the Mutiny, of the old relentless wars in which the original Kshatriyas are said to have wiped each other out completely, the violence began to emerge. It appeared in the disorders of 1942 and 1943, which this time his voice did not have the power to halt. It reappeared in August 1946, as if in macabre celebration of the fact that Nehru was about to head the first all-Indian government in Delhi as a prelude to complete independence. It began at Noakhali in eastern Bengal, where the Moslems killed the Hindus; it continued in Bihar, where the Hindus killed the Moslems. Gandhi went at once to Noakhali and walked barefoot from village to village, trying to still the violence. "Never in my life has the path been so uncertain and so dim before me," he said, and little light appeared as he went on his tragic pilgrimage, an old man in his late seventies, trying to staunch the bloodshed in Bengal, in Bihar, in Kashmir, in Calcutta, in Delhi, like an aged king going in penance to try and establish some lost realm of peace and human kindness. He won some notable successes, bringing the fraternization of Moslems and Hindus in Calcutta, but what he saw and what he heard seemed often to numb his reactions, so that when the Pakistanis invaded Kashmir, he did not protest at the sending of the Indian army there. Since he had given up hope of seeing India nonviolent, the first nation of *Satyagrahis*, it was better—he thought—to fight rather than to show cowardice.

Gandhi's efforts to protect the minority communities and end the massacres that attended partition like a doomful judgment merely increased the enmity of the fanatical. Moslems threatened his life in Noakhali, Hindus in Calcutta. He seemed to glory in the perils he was facing: "I seek my peace among disorders." And during his final days in Delhi, where he held his last great fast to bring the communities of the capital together, and succeeded where the police had failed in giving people of all groups at least some sense of security from murder, he felt violence drawing nearer to him, and the record of his last days is studded with remarks about his impending end that his followers tended to remember afterward as evidence of premonitory insight. It may have been no more than a realistic recognition of possibilities, for a bomb had exploded at one of his prayer meetings and he knew that Hindu extremists had designs on his life. But it may also have been a product of the willingness to sacrifice himself, a Christian rather than a Hindu preoccupation with martyrdom, that runs like a dark streak through his thoughts from his early manhood, merging at the end with the sense that immolation might give back a meaning that his life seemed to have lost in this time of horror and disappointment, when the India of which he had dreamed was turning into a land mutilated by political conflict and drenched in the literal blood of intolerance.

On the night before his death, according to his grand-niece Manubehn, he told her that if he were to die of sickness, she should tell the world he was a false Mahatma. "And if an explosion takes place, as it did last week, or if someone shot at me and I received his bullet in my bare chest without a sign and with Rama's name on my lips, only then should you say that I was a true Mahatma." The next day, January 30, 1948, at the hour before the nightfall when the winter sun in Delhi shines with a golden incandescence through an air faintly blue with the drifting smoke of newly lit dungfires, Gandhi, walking to his prayer meeting, was shot by a fellow Hindu and died calling on the name of Rama.

To many the coincidence will seem too neat. It is not

important. The important thing is that Gandhi died without anger and without fear, as he had taught, and that he died for what he had done and what he had been.

ix

It was on the day of Gandhi's death that the hopes that had come with the defeat of dictators and the collapse of empires seemed suddenly to darken. The world, one felt on hearing that news, had not changed after all. And Gandhi's associates seemed seized with a kind of insanity that made them act as if to prove that all he lived for had been irrelevant. The disposal of his body became the occasion for a vast state occasion, organized by the military authorities, a British general in immediate charge. Gandhi was taken on a weapons carrier to the place of samadhi beside the holy Jumna, with the Governor-General's bodyguard of lancers riding at the head of the procession, and thousands of soldiers, airmen, policemen, and sailors outnumbering the tiny group of *Satyagrahis* who walked near his body. Later, his bones were dropped from a military amphibious craft into the Ganges. His murderer was hanged under a law inherited from the British, and none of Gandhi's old comrades in the government was moved to protest that denial of his beliefs.

Yet it would take more than a military funeral and the execution of an assassin, more even than the political defeat that he saw in the partition of India, to turn Gandhi's career immediately into mere history. Long ago, in 1909, Tolstoi had remarked of the first *Satyagraha* campaign in South Africa that it was "the most important work now being done in the world." It was perhaps not an excessive estimate, if one applies Tolstoi's opinion to the totality of Gandhi's achievement, which can, with a simplification he might not have resented—for he was given to simplifying—be expressed in three items:

1. The recognition, before the Japanese had shown the physical vulnerability of European imperialism, that the liberation of colonial peoples could be achieved quickly, and without the self-defeating use of violence;

2. The demonstration, in a more thorough way than ever before, that nonviolent action is not merely, as others have shown, an effective means of resistance, but can also become the philosophic basis of a total reconstruction of society in such a way that excesses of power and violence are eliminated;

3. The demonstration that the individual, in co-operation with others and even on his own, can deploy a moral power that may result in changing the general mental climate and hence the political and social shape of the world.

We have all, in our ways of thinking, been changed by Gandhi's ideas and actions. This is not to say that even in India many people can be regarded as Gandhians, nor would he have wanted that. "There is no such thing as Gandhism," he once said, "and I do not want to leave any sect after me." What he did want to see was other men experimenting constantly with truth, and seeking the ways in which, within their own cultures to which he would have them remain loyal, moral lives can be lived. If there are Gandhian dogmas, they are few and simple: to practice nonviolence, which means also to simplify life until violence becomes unnecessary, and, by further implication, to approximate to physical equality while maintaining an infinite diversity of belief.

After Gandhi's example, it is unlikely to be forgotten that there is a viable revolutionary alternative to violent revolution, and in this sense our view of the possibilities of change has been extended; indeed, the very bitterness of the advocates of violence toward Gandhi shows that they realize the challenge he raises to their pretensions. In certain situations, since the liberation of India, Gandhi's methods have been used with success. They played a great part in the liberation of Ghana; they were the means by which American blacks made great advances toward equality and moved into militant self-respect—a fact that violent activists such as the Black Panthers have tried to obscure. In India itself, apart from Vinoba Bhave's Bhoodan movement for the redistribution of land, much of the reorganization of the country since Gandhi's death into linguistic states has been achieved by the use of methods he developed.

But, in most of these instances, it has been Gandhi's tactics that have been used rather than his greater strategy. Like his colleagues in Congress, most civil resisters have been concerned with gaining specific political goals by nonviolent means but have failed to proceed toward the general social transformation that might make violence less likely. The Indians make the distinction between *Satyagraha* and *Duragraha*, which is the force of stubbornness as opposed to the force of truth, and which can often amount to deliberate nonviolent coercion. Yet even coercive nonviolence is better than coercive violence, since it leaves the possibility of amendment; in any case, as I have suggested, the dividing line between coercion and persuasion in Gandhi's own fasts was very thin indeed. It may be impossible to live in society without exercising and experiencing some coercion; what Gandhi really taught were ways to make coercion relatively painless so that in the end, as with the British, something recognizably near to conversion may result.

In other respects Gandhi succeeded in modifying rather than fundamentally changing majority attitudes. Caste distinctions in India, for example, may have changed their forms since his campaigns against untouchability, but they have not vanished. It is no longer necessary for an untouchable in Kerala to stand sixty-four feet away from a Nambudiri Brahmin, as it was even thirty-five years ago; there are no longer people whom it is a pollution to see, as was once the case with a certain tribe of beggars in Travancore. Only occasionally does one now hear of villages where untouchables are forbidden to use the communal well. But in subtler ways the barriers remain. There are very few intermarriages between caste Hindus and untouchables, and an untouchable who rises by dint of education to a high government post will often find that while he is accepted at work with a bland official politeness, the homes of his colleagues are closed to him, and he lives in social isolation. The law forbids untouchability; in unpunishable ways custom maintains it.

Among the religious communities of India, Gandhi's achievements have been equally limited. Except for occasional minor outbursts, Hindus and Moslems now live together without fear, but they have not learned to love one another, and Moslems believe they are the victims of discrimination by a Hindu-dominated administration. A lasting truce rather than real peace is what Gandhi has created, but even that is better than lasting strife.

Because Gandhi was not a systematic thinker, it is hardly appropriate to subject his theories to systematic criticism. One judges him by his deeds, his experiments in the dynamics of personal relationships, his activist successes and failures. And in this realm it is clear that his virtues and his limitations were largely complementary. Because he had such a deep sense of the neglected potentialities of rural life, for example, he tended to ignore the realities of urban existence until, in the end, in Calcutta and Delhi, he was forced into the heart of them. In consequence, his social teachings made no real allowance for societies, like those in Europe, that were already industrialized and urbanized and were often condemned to be so by density of population. This may explain why Gandhian tactics were relatively successful when Martin Luther King used them in the still comparatively rural Southern states of America, but were much less effective when racial conflicts occurred in the wholly urban setting of Northern cities.

The area in which it is most usual to cast doubt on Gandhi's theories and methods is that of resistance to ruthless opponents. Could Gandhi have resisted Hitler, it is asked, as easily as he resisted Lord Irwin or even

Lord Willingdon? Could his proposal of wave after wave of *Satyagrahis* offering themselves for death really have succeeded against the armies of Japan?

Gandhi, indeed, had only a limited understanding of human mentalities that were remote from his own. His failure to make any impression on Jinnah was due to more than Jinnah's coldness; it derived just as much from Gandhi's inability to tune in with Jinnah's fears and aspirations. Similarly, because he could never imagine himself inside the mind of a Tamerlane, he could not believe there were men who would fail to respond to the moral force engendered by willing mass suffering; he was totally incapable of understanding Hitler, whom he insisted on regarding as misguided but fundamentally good and amenable to reason.

Gandhi's good fortune, in fact, was that until the last encounter he faced in action opponents whom he did understand. He developed an astonishing empathetic knowledge of the English view of life, and even evolved a personal code of chivalry that reflected one aspect of the class myth the sahibs cherished. Consider his remark about his opponent, Ambalal Sarabhai, in the Ahmedabad strike: "His resolute will and transparent sincerity were wonderful and captured my heart. It was a pleasure to be pitched against him." Gandhi almost certainly felt that it was also a pleasure to be "pitched" against Lord Irwin, and the pleasure may well have been reciprocated. But pleasure to be pitched against Hitler? The imagination hardly admits it.

It was perhaps Gandhi's knowledge of the British, and his skillful use of their concepts of decency as levers to move their consciences, that made him so much the man for the time in India. He appears, indeed, to have understood the British better than he understood his fellow Indians, for in the end the British behaved as he had always believed they would, but the Indians revealed depths of violence he had not dared to imagine.

Like any of us, Gandhi hated to admit that there were circumstances in which the belief he had made the cornerstone of his life would be inapplicable, and this led him to a few extravagant and foolish statements. For example, he was asked, not long before his death, how he would deal with an attack by atom bomb. "I will not go underground, I will not go into shelter," he said. "I will come out in the open and let the pilot see I have not a trace of evil against him. The pilot will not see our faces from his great height, I know. But the longing in our hearts that he will not come to harm would reach up to him and his eyes would be opened." In a man so lacking in naïveté as Gandhi, such an answer was an oblique admission that he had no answer.

On the other hand, there is more to be said than his critics have admitted for his recommendation of non-violent resistance to dictators and ruthless invaders. The point surely is that these are situations that are almost hopeless in immediate terms, and that violent resistance is likely to be as ineffective in the short run as non-violent resistance. One has to wait until the totalitarian regime or foreign rule begins to decay internally. Then the effect of stubborn and apparently useless resistance may be made manifest. And in this long run, nonviolent resistance is probably the more effective. It is likely that Tolstoi's one-man nonviolent moral defiance did more to erode the resolve of the Tsarist regime than all the terrorist acts of the Narodnaya Volya. It is also probable that the one resistance to Hitler that succeeded by its own power was the nonviolent noncooperation campaign of Norwegian teachers against the Nazification of education in their country. The more celebrated violent resistance movements survived only because Germany was at war and aid could be got from its enemy, and they had real success only when they emerged as irregular auxiliaries to the Allied Forces. It is an illusion that in the modern world violent revolutionaries can unaided overthrow any strong government.

During World War II, Gandhi aroused much attention by urging the Jews to take the course of nonviolent resistance against the Nazis. What appalled him even more than the physical destruction of the Jews was the devastation of their self-respect. "The Jews should have offered themselves to the butcher's knife," he said. "They should have thrown themselves into the sea from cliffs. . . . It would have aroused the world and the people of Germany."

One has to remember that Gandhi was relatively unconcerned about death, but deeply concerned about the way of dying. "Death is never sweet," he said on another occasion, "not even if it is suffered for the highest ideal. It remains unspeakably bitter, and still it can be the utmost assertion of our individuality." It was in this sense that he thought of the Jews; if they were to die, he believed, it was better to go asserting their individualities in nonviolent resistance than allowing themselves to be taken to the slaughter like cattle. Despite the extravagant way he expressed himself, Gandhi's argument was not without logic. For if, at the beginning of their persecution, the Jews of Germany and Austria had resisted with sufficient drama they might not have survived—they did not survive in any case—but they would have made the world less ready to find excuses for Hitler and might have started a swell of sympathy, a beginning of resistance among the German people. It it just conceivable, moreover, that such tactics might have obliged the Nazis to let more Jews out of Germany and that lives would thus have been saved.

There is an underlying shrewdness in Gandhi's arguments. One can rarely dismiss them entirely as the wanderings of an eccentric fancy. They are the products of a mind trained not to evade any question but to seek always a moral answer. Where Gandhi was extravagantly wrong, it was usually from ignorance of the facts rather than from bad judgment. And the most important fact, of which he was almost willfully ignorant, was the extent and the reality of evil. He could never admit that the end of sorrow was less than love.

SHORT BIBLIOGRAPHY
INDEX

SHORT BIBLIOGRAPHY

Andrews, C. F. (ed.). *Mahatma Gandhi at Work.* New York: Macmillan, 1931.
———. *Mahatma Gandhi's Ideas.* New York: Macmillan, 1930.
Ashe, Geoffrey. *Gandhi: A Study in Revolution.* New York: Stein and Day, 1968.
Bondurant, Joan V. *Conquest of Violence: The Gandhian Philosophy of Conflict.* Rev. ed. Berkeley, Calif.: University of California Press, 1968.
Bose, Nirmal Kumar. *Gandhi in Indian Politics.* Bombay: Lalvani Publishing House, 1967.
———. *My Days with Gandhi.* Calcutta: Nishana, 1953.
Brecher, Michael. *Nehru, a Political Biography.* Boston: Beacon Press, 1962.
Catlin, George. *In the Path of Mahatma Gandhi.* Chicago: Regnery, 1950.
Datta, Dhirendra Mohan. *The Philosophy of Mahatma Gandhi.* Madison, Wis.: University of Wisconsin Press, 1953.
Dhawan, Gopinath. *The Political Philosophy of Mahatma*

Gandhi. 3rd. rev. ed. Ahmedabad: Navajivan Publishing House, 1952.

Erikson, Erik H. *Gandhi's Truth: On the Origins of Militant Nonviolence*. New York: W. W. Norton, 1969.

Fischer, Louis. *The Life of Mahatma Gandhi*. New York: Harper & Brothers, 1950.

Gandhi, M. K. *An Autobiography of the Story of My Experiments with Truth*. 2 vols. New York: Macmillan, 1927, 1929.

―――. *Collected Works*. In progress, commencing 1956. (The *Collected Works*, of which more than twenty volumes have already been published by the Government of India, will be the definitive source of Gandhi's writings; it is estimated that there will eventually be sixty volumes.)

―――. *Hind Swaraj* (1909). Rev. ed. Ahmedabad: Navajivan Publishing House, 1946.

―――. *Hindu Dharma*. Ahmedabad: Navajivan Publishing House, 1950.

―――. *Non-violence in Peace and War*. 2 vols. Ahmedabad: Navajivan Publishing House, 1942, 1949.

―――. *Non-Violent Resistance* (originally published in 1935 as *Satyagraha*). New York: Schocken Books, 1961.

―――. *Satyagraha in South Africa*. Madras: S. Ganeson, 1928.

Jack, Homer A. (ed.). *The Gandhi Reader*. Bloomington, Ind.: Indiana University Press, 1961.

Merton, Thomas (ed.). *Gandhi on Non-Violence*. New York: New Directions, 1964.

Muzumdar, Haridas T. *Gandhi against the Empire*. New York: Universal Publishing, 1932.

Nag, Kalidas. *Tolstoy and Gandhi*. New York: William S. Heinman, 1950.

Nanda, B. R. *Mahatma Gandhi*. Boston: Beacon Press, 1958.

Nehru, Jawaharlal. *Toward Freedom: An Autobiography*. New York: John Day, 1942.

Pyarelal, Nair. *Mahatma Gandhi: The Early Phase*. Ahmedabad: Navajivan Publishing House, 1965.

―――. *Mahatma Gandhi: The Last Phase*. 2 vols. Ahmedabad: Navajivan Publishing House, 1956, 1958.

Reynolds, Reginald. *A Quest for Gandhi*. New York: Double-
day, 1952.
Rolland, Romain. *Mahatma Gandhi*. New York and London:
Century, 1924.
Shahani, Ranjee. *Mr. Gandhi*. New York: Macmillan, 1961.
Tendulkar, D. G. *Gandhi in Champaran*. New Delhi: Publi-
cation Division, Ministry of Information and Broadcasting,
Government of India.
————. *Mahatma*. 8 vols. Bombay: V. K. Jhaveri and D. G.
Tendulkar, 1951–54.
Woodcock, George. *Civil Disobedience*.
Toronto, Canada: Canadian Broadcasting Corp., 1966.

INDEX

- Passive Resistance -

w/out surprises ~~simple~~
no fear.
people are watching

DID HE SUCEED?

Got Brittan out of India

Chg public opinion

Lessen the caste system

Salt March. March to the sea

Central to lives of people

Many people involved

(Never been done before?)

Identify w/ some larger
goal - God!

Followers - organized
Not spontaneous.
nothing illegal

- Talks universal - ideals.

no volunteers - Violence might occur

no force Non coercive

longer involved - feel more right

Pol & Moral Victory - achieve w/out failure, kills lives

Other side → might be won over